C000257752

Cycle TOURS

Norfolk and Suffolk

Nick Cotton

First published in 2002 by
Philip's, a division of
Octopus Publishing Group Ltd
2-4 Heron Quays
London E14 4JP

First edition 2002
Second impression 2005

Based on the original Ordnance Survey Cycle Tours series
first published by Philip's and Ordnance Survey®.

ISBN 0-540-08197-3

The route maps in this book are reproduced from
Ordnance Survey® Landranger® mapping.

Text and compilation copyright © Philip's 2002

This product includes mapping data licensed from Ordnance
Survey® with the permission of the Controller of Her Majesty's
Stationery Office. © Crown copyright 2002. All rights reserved.
Licence number 100011710

Printed and bound in Spain by Cayfosa-Quebecor

Photographic acknowledgements

AA Photo Library 39, 52, 63, 93, 119, 125, 126 • Nick Cotton
64, 73, 81, 85, 109, 111 • Derek Forss 27, 69, 103 • Judy Todd
13, 19, 36, 46, 57, 75, 105

Contents

Abbreviations and symbols

Directions

L	left
R	right
LH	left-hand
RH	right-hand
SA	straight ahead or straight across
T-j	T-junction, a junction where you have to give way
X-roads	crossroads, a junction where you may or may not have to give way
'Placename 2'	words in quotation marks are those that appear on signposts; the numbers indicate distance in miles unless stated otherwise

Distance and grade

The number of drink bottles indicates the grade:

🍶 Easy
🍶🍶🍶 Moderate
🍶🍶🍶🍶🍶 Strenuous

The grade is based on the amount of climbing involved.

Refreshments

Pubs and teashops on or near the route are listed. The tankard 🍺 symbols indicate pubs particularly liked by the author.

Page diagrams

The page diagrams on the introductory pages show how the map pages have been laid out, how they overlap and if any inset maps have been used.

This section of the route is shown on pages 20 and 21

This overlap area appears at the foot of pages 20 and 21 and at the top of pages 22 and 23

This section of the route is shown on pages 22 and 23

This area is shown as an inset on page 21

Richmond

Cross-profiles

The vertical scale is the same on each diagram but the horizontal scale varies according to the length of the route.

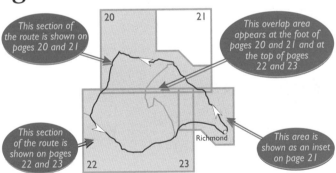

Sychnant Pass

Cefn Coch

Rowen

Start/finish

Start/finish

Legend to 1:50 000 maps

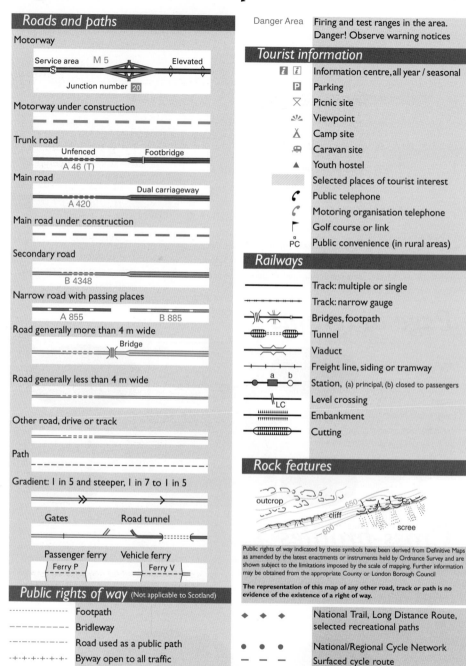

Roads and paths

Motorway

Service area (S)   M 5   Elevated
Junction number 20

Motorway under construction

Trunk road
Unfenced   Footbridge
A 46 (T)

Main road
Dual carriageway
A 420

Main road under construction

Secondary road
B 4348

Narrow road with passing places
A 855   B 885

Road generally more than 4 m wide
Bridge

Road generally less than 4 m wide

Other road, drive or track

Path

Gradient: 1 in 5 and steeper, 1 in 7 to 1 in 5

Gates   Road tunnel

Passenger ferry   Vehicle ferry
Ferry P   Ferry V

Public rights of way (Not applicable to Scotland)

.... Footpath
— — — — — Bridleway
—·—·—·—·— Road used as a public path
–+–+–+–+–+– Byway open to all traffic

Danger Area   Firing and test ranges in the area. Danger! Observe warning notices

Tourist information

🅸 ⓘ	Information centre, all year / seasonal
🅿	Parking
✕	Picnic site
☼	Viewpoint
Å	Camp site
⛺	Caravan site
▲	Youth hostel
▨	Selected places of tourist interest
☎	Public telephone
☎	Motoring organisation telephone
⚑	Golf course or link
PC	Public convenience (in rural areas)

Railways

Track: multiple or single
Track: narrow gauge
Bridges, footpath
Tunnel
Viaduct
Freight line, siding or tramway
Station, (a) principal, (b) closed to passengers
Level crossing
Embankment
Cutting

Rock features

outcrop   650   cliff   –600   scree

Public rights of way indicated by these symbols have been derived from Definitive Maps as amended by the latest enactments or instruments held by Ordnance Survey and are shown subject to the limitations imposed by the scale of mapping. Further information may be obtained from the appropriate County or London Borough Council

The representation of this map of any other road, track or path is no evidence of the existence of a right of way.

◆ ◆ ◆   National Trail, Long Distance Route, selected recreational paths

● ● ●   National/Regional Cycle Network

— — —   Surfaced cycle route

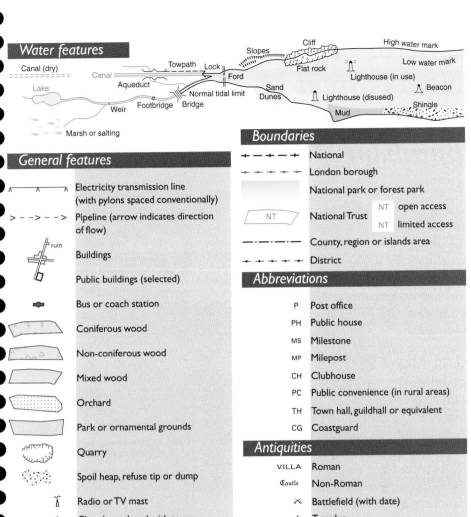

Water features

Canal (dry)
Canal
Aqueduct
Lake
Towpath Lock
Ford
Normal tidal limit
Weir Footbridge Bridge
Marsh or salting

Cliff High water mark
Slopes Low water mark
Flat rock
Lighthouse (in use)
Sand Dunes Lighthouse (disused) Beacon
Mud Shingle

General features

	Electricity transmission line (with pylons spaced conventionally)
> – –> – –>	Pipeline (arrow indicates direction of flow)
ruin	Buildings
	Public buildings (selected)
	Bus or coach station
	Coniferous wood
	Non-coniferous wood
	Mixed wood
	Orchard
	Park or ornamental grounds
	Quarry
	Spoil heap, refuse tip or dump
	Radio or TV mast
	Church or chapel with tower
	Church or chapel with spire
+	Church or chapel without tower or spire
○	Chimney or tower
	Glasshouse
+	Graticule intersection at 5' intervals
Ⓗ	Heliport
△	Triangulation pillar
	Windmill with or without sails
	Windpump

Boundaries

+ – + – +	National
–○– ○– ○– ○–	London borough
	National park or forest park
NT	National Trust NT open access NT limited access
—·—·—	County, region or islands area
+ + + +	District

Abbreviations

P	Post office
PH	Public house
MS	Milestone
MP	Milepost
CH	Clubhouse
PC	Public convenience (in rural areas)
TH	Town hall, guildhall or equivalent
CG	Coastguard

Antiquities

VILLA	Roman
Castle	Non-Roman
✗	Battlefield (with date)
☆	Tumulus
+	Position of antiquity which cannot be drawn to scale
ℳ	Ancient monuments and historic buildings in the care of the Secretaries of State for the Environment, for Scotland and for Wales and that are open to the public

Heights

—50—	Contours are at 10 metres vertical interval
·144	Heights are to the nearest metre above mean sea level

Heights shown close to a triangulation pillar refer to the station height at ground level and not necessarily to the summit

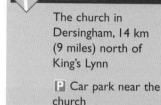

Across northwest Norfolk from Sandringham to Burnham Market

Start

The church in Dersingham, 14 km (9 miles) north of King's Lynn

P Car park near the church

Distance and grade

55 km (34 miles)

Easy

Terrain

Gently rolling arable land. Mixture of sandstone and flint houses. Lowest point – 7m (23 ft) just west of Burnham Market. Highest point – 80 m (262 ft) at North Pole Farm near Houghton Park (6)

Nearest Railway

King's Lynn, 13km (8 miles) south of the route at Sandringham

In the gently rolling land of the northwest corner of Norfolk through which this ride takes you, there is a division in the materials used for the construction of the older dwellings. To the west there is a high incidence of the dark yellow sandstone known as Norfolk Ragstone, used even when the individual stones are very small. Further east the old buildings are almost exclusively red-brick, flint or a combination of both. The ride starts by heading east away from the royal residence of Sandringham between attractive lines of beech and copper beech trees. The route turns north by Houghton Hall towards Burnham Market – an attractive village with interesting craft and antique shops. A quiet lane heads east to Ringstead where there is a tearoom at the Post Office and an excellent pub. South of Ringstead you may wish to make a diversion to visit the lavender fields at Heacham. Otherwise the route avoids the busy A149 by following quiet lanes through Sedgeford and Ingoldisthorpe to return to Dersingham.

Dersingham Anmer New Houghton Bagthorpe Stanhoe Burnham Market Choseley Farm Ringstead Sedgeford Ingoldisthorpe

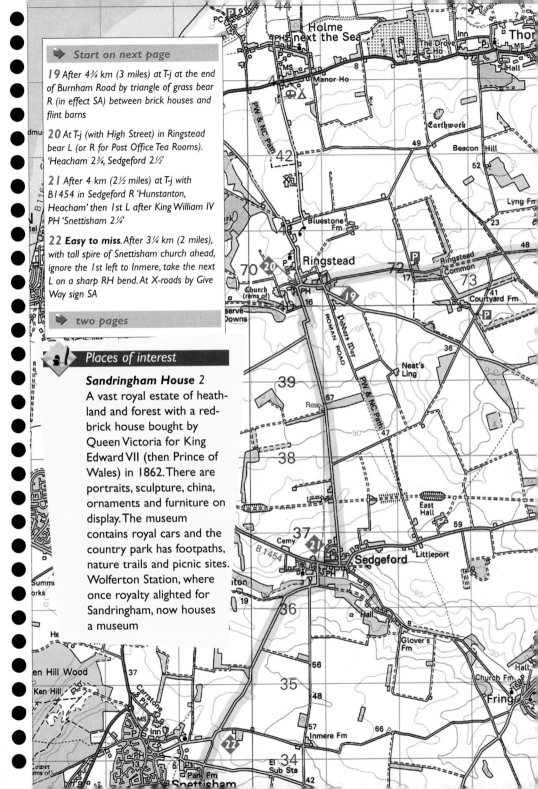

➡ **Start on next page**

19 After 4¾ km (3 miles) at T-j at the end of Burnham Road by triangle of grass bear R (in effect SA) between brick houses and flint barns

20 At T-j (with High Street) in Ringstead bear L (or R for Post Office Tea Rooms). 'Heacham 2¾, Sedgeford 2½'

21 After 4 km (2½ miles) at T-j with B1454 in Sedgeford R 'Hunstanton, Heacham' then 1st L after King William IV PH 'Snettisham 2¼'

22 Easy to miss. After 3¼ km (2 miles), with tall spire of Snettisham church ahead, ignore the 1st left to Inmere, take the next L on a sharp RH bend. At X-roads by Give Way sign SA

➡ **two pages**

⬧ Places of interest

Sandringham House 2
A vast royal estate of heathland and forest with a red-brick house bought by Queen Victoria for King Edward VII (then Prince of Wales) in 1862. There are portraits, sculpture, china, ornaments and furniture on display. The museum contains royal cars and the country park has footpaths, nature trails and picnic sites. Wolferton Station, where once royalty alighted for Sandringham, now houses a museum

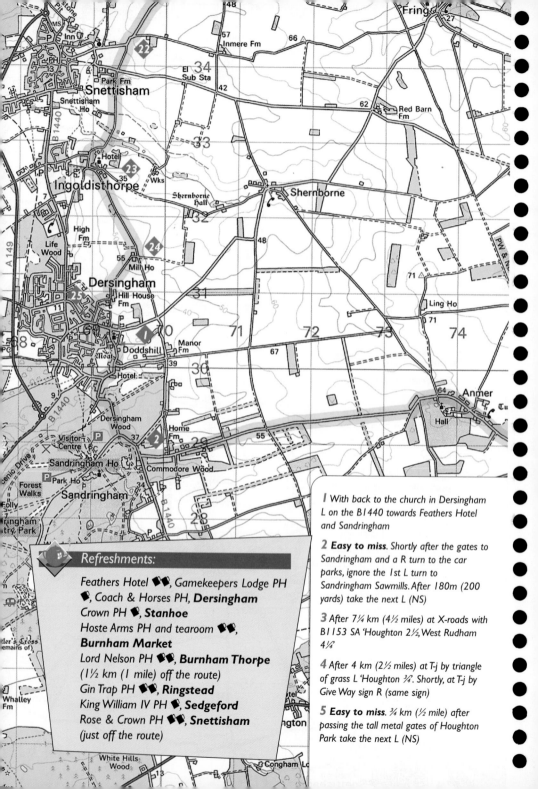

Refreshments:

Feathers Hotel 🍴🍴, Gamekeepers Lodge PH 🍴, Coach & Horses PH, **Dersingham**

Crown PH 🍴, **Stanhoe**

Hoste Arms PH and tearoom 🍴🍴, **Burnham Market**

Lord Nelson PH 🍴🍴, **Burnham Thorpe** (1½ km (1 mile) off the route)

Gin Trap PH 🍴🍴, **Ringstead**

King William IV PH 🍴, **Sedgeford**

Rose & Crown PH 🍴🍴, **Snettisham** (just off the route)

1 With back to the church in Dersingham L on the B1440 towards Feathers Hotel and Sandringham

2 **Easy to miss.** Shortly after the gates to Sandringham and a R turn to the car parks, ignore the 1st L turn to Sandringham Sawmills. After 180m (200 yards) take the next L (NS)

3 After 7¼ km (4½ miles) at X-roads with B1153 SA 'Houghton 2½, West Rudham 4¼'

4 After 4 km (2½ miles) at T-j by triangle of grass L 'Houghton ¾'. Shortly, at T-j by Give Way sign R (same sign)

5 **Easy to miss.** ¾ km (½ mile) after passing the tall metal gates of Houghton Park take the next L (NS)

6 At X-roads by the brick and flint barns of North Pole Farm SA (NS)

7 At X-roads by Give Way sign and triangle of grass L (NS)

8 At X-roads by triangle of grass shortly after small flint church in Bagthorpe SA (NS)

9 At X-roads (with busy B1454) SA 'Barwick 1'

 next page

22 Easy to miss. After 3¼ km (2 miles), with tall spire of Snettisham church ahead, ignore the 1st L to Inmere, take the next L on a sharp RH bend. At X-roads by Give Way sign SA

23 At T-j with Shernborne Road L

24 Easy to miss. After 1½ km (1 miles), shortly after brow of hill 1st R by triangle of grass and houses with neat hedges

25 At T-j in Dersingham at the bottom of the hill L (NS) and follow the road back to the start

10 At T-j (with B1155) by Give Way sign R. At T-j with Burnham Road by the pond in Stanhoe R 'Wells 10, Burnham Market 4'

11 1¼ km (¾ mile) after the Crown PH in Stanhoe next R 'North Creake 2'

12 After 1½ km (1 mile) 1st L at X-roads in the middle of brick and flint farm buildings 'Burnham Market'. Sea views

13 At T-j (with B1355) at the end of Beacon Hill Road L. At T-j with Front Street by the Lord Nelson PH L '6ft 6ins width limit'

14 At T-j by the memorial cross in the centre of Burnham Market turn L towards the church

15 Towards the end of the village 1st R 'Brancaster 2' then immediately L onto Ringstead Road

16 After 4¾ km (3 miles) at X-roads by Give Way sign SA (NS)

17 At X-roads with B1153 SA 'Ringstead 4'

18 At T-j by Give Way sign with Xmas Cottage ahead R then 1st L

◄ three pages

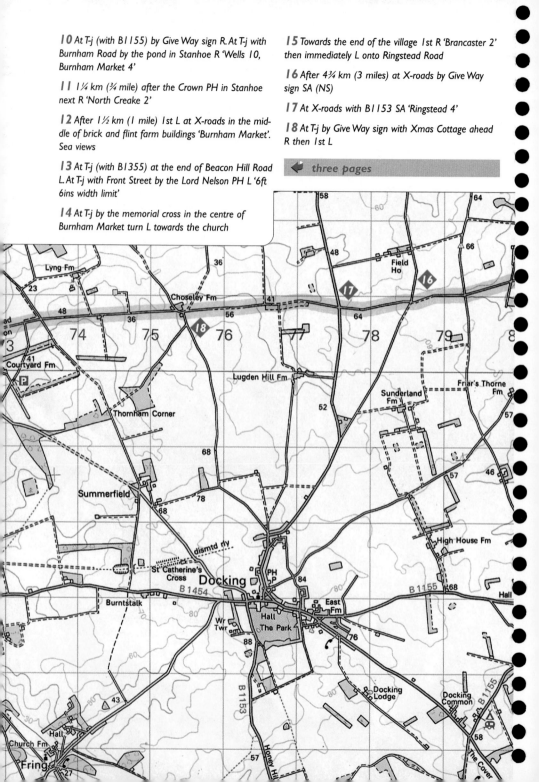

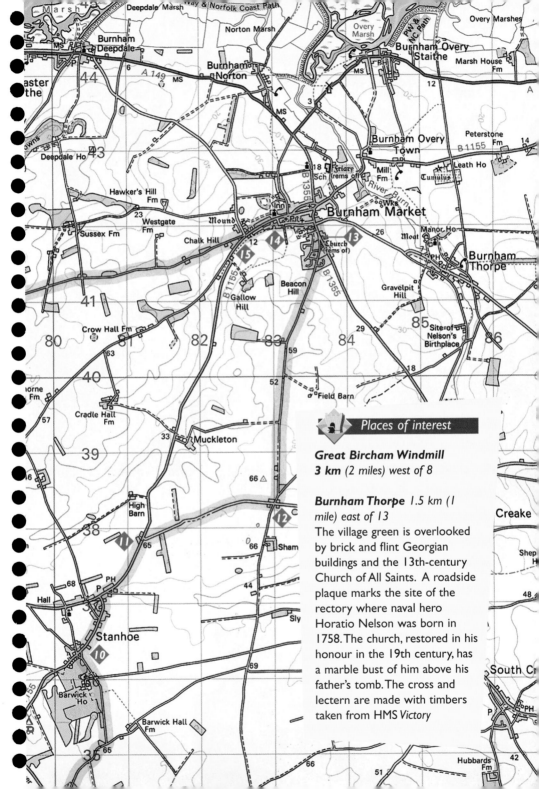

Places of interest

Great Bircham Windmill
3 km *(2 miles) west of 8*

Burnham Thorpe *1.5 km (1 mile) east of 13*
The village green is overlooked by brick and flint Georgian buildings and the 13th-century Church of All Saints. A roadside plaque marks the site of the rectory where naval hero Horatio Nelson was born in 1758. The church, restored in his honour in the 19th century, has a marble bust of him above his father's tomb. The cross and lectern are made with timbers taken from HMS *Victory*

North from Fakenham to the coast at Wells-next-the-Sea

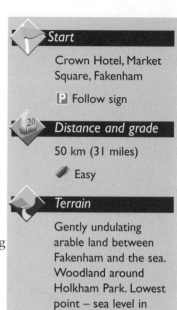

Start

Crown Hotel, Market Square, Fakenham

P Follow sign

Distance and grade

50 km (31 miles)

Easy

Terrain

Gently undulating arable land between Fakenham and the sea. Woodland around Holkham Park. Lowest point – sea level in Wells. Highest point – 66 m (220 ft) to the east of North Creake

This ride heads west then north to the coast at Wells-next-the-Sea, returning via Little Walsingham and Great Snoring. The ride starts by following the valley of the River Wensum, one of the four main rivers draining the east of Norfolk, all linking at Great Yarmouth. You pass fine round-towered flint churches in Shereford and Syderstone as you cross a gently rolling arable landscape, passing copses of broadleaf woodland, particularly in the stream and river valleys. A short, unavoidable section of busy road (the B1355) links the attractive flint villages of South and North Creake before the ride turns northeast, climbing to its highpoint at 66 m (220 ft) with fine views of the triumphal arch of Holkham Hall. A long, gentle, wooded descent leads down into Wells and a bustling waterfront. If you had coffee in North Creake and lunch in Wells, then it only remains to take tea in Little Walsingham, a charming village with a distinctly religious feel boasting a priory, an abbey and a shrine dedicated to the Virgin Mary.

Fakenham   Hempton   Shereford   Coxford   Syderstone   South Creake   North Creake   New Holkh

Places of interest

South Creake 12

The village has one of East Anglia's finest churches, dating mainly from the 13th and 14th centuries. The medieval hammerbeam roof is decorated with carved angels. An unusual brass depicts a priest lying between his parents. The nave, 15th-century rood screen and pulpit are all magnificent

North Creake 13

Changing styles are reflected in St Mary's Church, founded in 1300, with the faded 'Doom' painting over the chancel arch, the Royal Arms of Charles I above the north door and a tasteful 1978 memorial chapel. Fragments of the old abbey remain – it had to close when the resident canons died in the 1504 plague

▲ Wells-next-the-Sea

Refreshments:

Lots of choice in **Fakenham**
Lynn Arms PH, **Syderstone**
Jolly Farmers PH 🍴, tearoom, **North Creake**
Crown PH 🍴🍴, Ark Royal PH 🍴, Lifeboat PH 🍴, lots of choice in **Wells**
Three Horseshoes PH 🍴🍴, **Warham**
The Bull PH 🍴, Robin Hood Inn, **Walsingham**

Golden Gates   Wells-next-the-Sea   Warham   Wighton   Great Walsingham   Little Walsingham   Great Snoring

1 With back to the Crown Hotel in the Market Square, Fakenham, R onto Bridge Street 'Dereham B1146, Swaffham (A1065)

2 Cross the river. At X-roads (your priority) shortly after the end of the houses in Hempton turn R 'King's Lynn, Cromer A148'. At offset X-roads with A1065 SA 'Dunton 4, Shereford 2'

3 Through Shereford. ¾ km (½ mile) after the round flint church tower 1st R 'Dunton, Tatterford 1½'

4 Cross bridge over river then take the 1st L 'Tatterford'

5 At T-j L (NS) then after ¾ km (½ mile) 1st R 'Tattersett'

6 At T-j bear R (in effect SA) 'Broomsthorpe, Tattersett'

7 Follow road round to the R and signs for Tattersett

8 At X-roads with the A148 L then 1st L opposite garage. After ½ km (¼ mile) 1st R then at X-roads with A148 SA 'Tattersett'

9 At T-j with B1454 L 'Docking 6, Heacham 11' then 1st R 'Syderstone'

10 After ¾ km (½ mile) 1st L 'Syderstone ¾'

I I At T-j by the church in Syderstone L then 1st R 'South Creake 3'

➡️ *next page*

26 At 1st X-roads in Great Snoring (your priority) SA 'Fakenham'. At 2nd X-roads (also your priority) by telephone box and Great Snoring village sign R 'Unsuitable for HGVs'

27 After 4¾ km (3 miles) at roundabout with A148 3rd exit 'King's Lynn' (**take care** – busy road) then after 18m (20 yards) leave main road and bear

diagonally L onto narrow tarmac path. After 180m (200 yards) 1st L

28 At X-roads at the end of Thorpland Road SA onto Holt Road 'Fakenham Town Centre'

29 At T-j in the centre of Fakenham R onto Norwich Street (one way street) to return to the Market Square

12 After 4¾ km (3 miles) at T-j with B1355 in South Creake L 'Burnham Market 4'

13 Busy 2½ km (1½ miles) section. Go past church in North Creake and take the second R by telephone box onto Wells Road

14 Steady climb over 3¼ km (2 miles). At X-roads at the top of hill (arch to the left) L 'Wells 3½'

15 After 4 km (2½ miles) at T-j with B1105 L 'Wells'

16 After 2 km (1¼ miles) **ignore** 1st right to Hunstanton (A149). After further ½ km (¼ mile) take the next R 'Beach, Town Centre' then immediately L 'Beach, Car Park'

17 At T-j (with B1105) turn R along seafront and follow road round to the R

18 At T-j with Warham Road (A149) L 'Cromer' then R 'Warham, Wighton'

19 After 2½ km (1½ miles) 1st L 'Warham ½'

20 At X-roads by the Horseshoes PH in Warham R 'Wighton'

21 Lovely sunken lane, high hedgerows. At T-j by a triangle of grass and Give Way sign L then 1st R 'Walsingham'

22 At T-j (with B1388) R then R again by the telephone box 'Unbridged ford'. 1st L by memorial stone

23 At X-roads at the end of St Peters Road L. At T-j with a high flint wall ahead R 'Parking'

24 At T-j by brick lock-up at the end of square L then after 360 m (400 yards) 1st L onto Church Street

25 Go past church. At X-roads by Give Way sign R 'Great Snoring, Thursford'

26 At 1st X-roads in Great Snoring (your priority) SA 'Fakenham'. At 2nd X-roads (also your priority) by telephone box and Great Snoring village sign R 'Unsuitable for HGVs'

◀ previous page

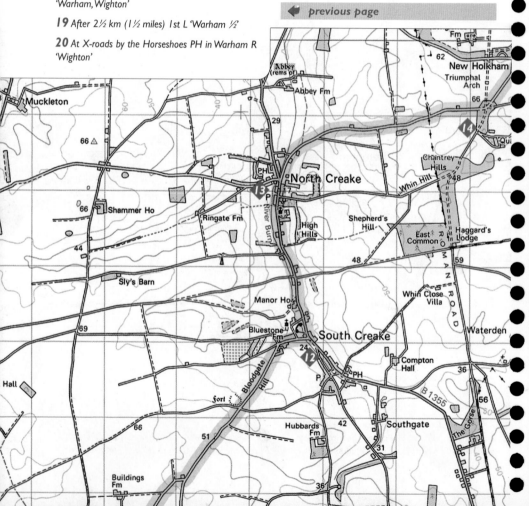

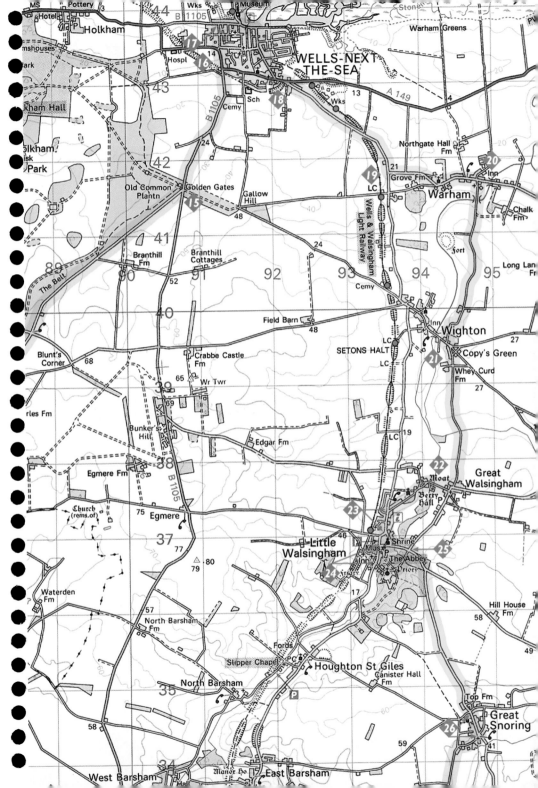

Northeast from Fakenham to the coast at Blakeney and Cley

The start of this links Fakenham with the coast and then passes through the curiously named village of Great Snoring and the attractions of Little Walsingham with its abbey, priory and pretty flint houses. At Wighton, it turns northeast towards the coast at Stiffkey ('Stooky') Blakeney and Cley ('Cly'), all bird-watching sites *par excellence*. The ride turns south, following the wooded valley of the River Glaven to Hunworth before entering the maze of tiny farm lanes south of Briston. Just 5 km (3 miles) west of Briston is the one point in Norfolk where the land rises above the 100 metre contour line, near the junction of the B1354 and B1110.

Start

The Crown Hotel, Market Square, Fakenham

🅿 Follow signs

Distance and grade

66 km (41 miles)

🖌 Easy

Terrain

Gently undulating arable land. Broadleaf copses. Coastline at Blakeney and Cley. Lowest point – sea level at Blakeney and Cley. Highest point – 77 m (253 ft) just west of Stibbard (30)

Refreshments

Lots of choice in **Fakenham**
Bull Inn 🍴, Robin Hood Inn, **Little Walsingham**
Red Lion PH 🍴🍴, **Stiffkey** (just north of the route at 12)
Bluebell PH, **Langham**
Kings Arms PH 🍴🍴, White Horse PH 🍴🍴, lots of choice in **Blakeney**
George & Dragon PH 🍴, Three Swallows PH 🍴🍴, **Cley next the Sea**
Kings Head PH 🍴, **Letheringsett**
Hunny Bell PH 🍴🍴, **Hunworth**
John Stracey PH 🍴, **Briston**
Boar Inn 🍴, **Great Ryburgh**

Fakenham   Great Snoring   Little Walsingham   Great Walsingham   Wighton   Stiffkey   Langham   Blakeney   Cley next the Sea   Glandford

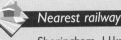

Nearest railway

Sheringham, 11km (6¾ miles) east of Cley next the Sea

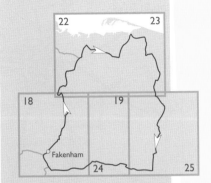

Places of interest

Fakenham 1

This attractive market town dates from Saxon times and was a Royal Manor until the 17th century. Its Market Place has two old coaching inns both showing traces of earlier work behind Georgian façades, and the parish church has a commanding 15th-century tower

Little Walsingham 24

A village with tall timbered houses lying in a woodland setting. It was a medieval place of pilgrimage noted for the Shrine of Virgin Mary, founded in the 11th century. The Augustinian friary and the Franciscan Priory were added later. The priory ruins are approached by a 15th-century gateway in the High Street

▼ Cley next the Sea

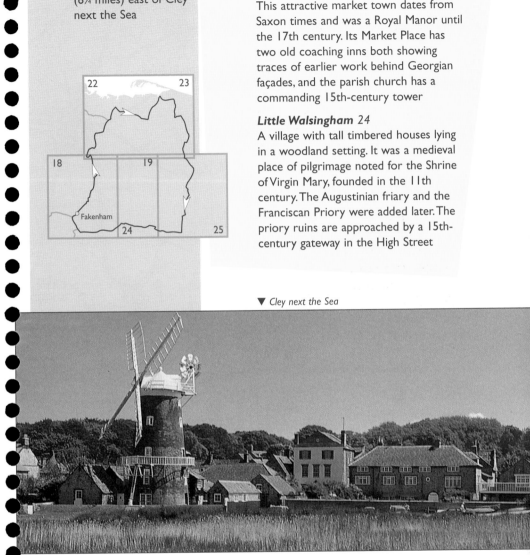

Letheringsett   Hunworth   Briston   Nethergate   Wood Norton   Stibbard   Great Ryburgh

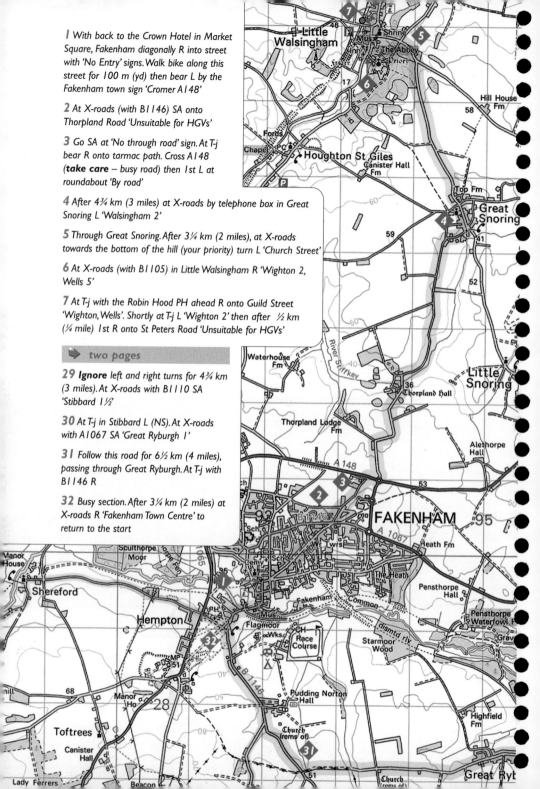

1 With back to the Crown Hotel in Market Square, Fakenham diagonally R into street with 'No Entry' signs. Walk bike along this street for 100 m (yd) then bear L by the Fakenham town sign 'Cromer A148'

2 At X-roads (with B1146) SA onto Thorpland Road 'Unsuitable for HGVs'

3 Go SA at 'No through road' sign. At T-j bear R onto tarmac path. Cross A148 (**take care** – busy road) then 1st L at roundabout 'By road'

4 After 4¾ km (3 miles) at X-roads by telephone box in Great Snoring L 'Walsingham 2'

5 Through Great Snoring. After 3¼ km (2 miles), at X-roads towards the bottom of the hill (your priority) turn L 'Church Street'

6 At X-roads (with B1105) in Little Walsingham R 'Wighton 2, Wells 5'

7 At T-j with the Robin Hood PH ahead R onto Guild Street 'Wighton, Wells'. Shortly at T-j L 'Wighton 2' then after ½ km (¼ mile) 1st R onto St Peters Road 'Unsuitable for HGVs'

↪ **two pages**

29 **Ignore** left and right turns for 4¾ km (3 miles). At X-roads with B1110 SA 'Stibbard 1½'

30 At T-j in Stibbard L (NS). At X-roads with A1067 SA 'Great Ryburgh 1'

31 Follow this road for 6½ km (4 miles), passing through Great Ryburgh. At T-j with B1146 R

32 Busy section. After 3¼ km (2 miles) at X-roads R 'Fakenham Town Centre' to return to the start

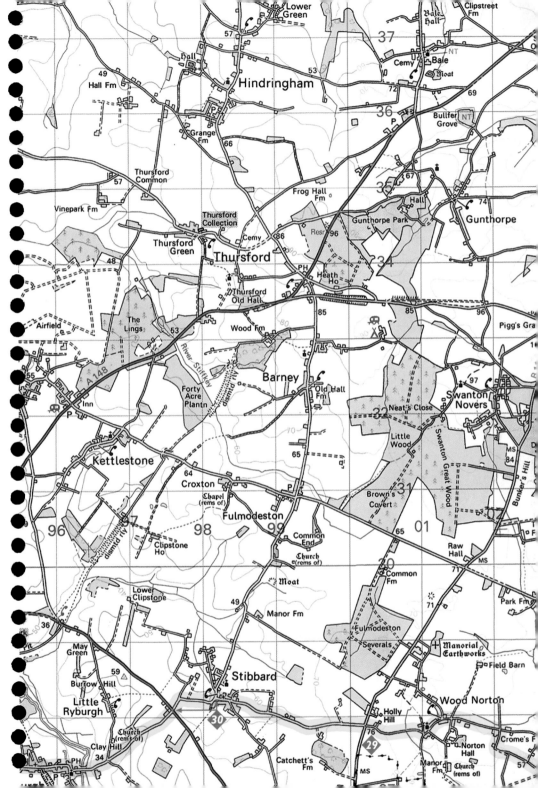

8 At T-j by memorial cross and triangle of grass bear R (in effect SA). At T-j by telephone box L 'Binham 3' then 1st L (NS)

9 After 2½ km (1½ miles) 1st R in Wighton. At X-roads SA 'Binham, Holt' then at T-j R

10 After 1¼ km (¾ mile) 1st L by Nutwood Farm 'Warham 2, Stiffkey 2½'

11 At X-roads SA 'Stiffkey'

12 At T-j (sea views) L to visit Stiffkey or R for continu-ation of route 'Cockthorpe 1, Binham 2, Langham 2½'

13 After 4 km (2½ miles) at T-j (with B1388) L 'Blakeney 2½'. Shortly after the Bluebell PH 1st L 'Blakeney B1388'

14 At X-roads with A149 SA onto Westgate Street 'Blakeney Quay' then 1st R after Blakeney Hotel onto High Street

15 At the end of High Street, at X-roads with A149 L 'Cromer'

16 This 1½ km (1 miles) section may be busy. Use the pavement with discretion. After crossing river, on sharp LH bend follow main road to the L to visit Cley or turn R here for continuation of route 'Car Park. Church'

17 After 1¼ km (¾ mile), 1st R by Three Swallows PH 'Wiveton 1, Glandford 1½'

18 At X-roads SA 'Glandford'

19 After 5¾ km (3½ miles) at X-roads with A148 SA 'Water Mill' and follow road round to the R over bridge. At X-roads L 'Thornage 2, Melton Constable 4'

20 After 1¼ km (¾ mile) 1st L 'Hunworth, Briston'

➡ **three pages**

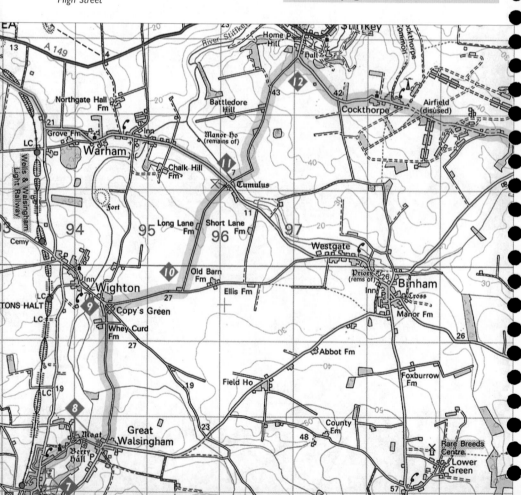

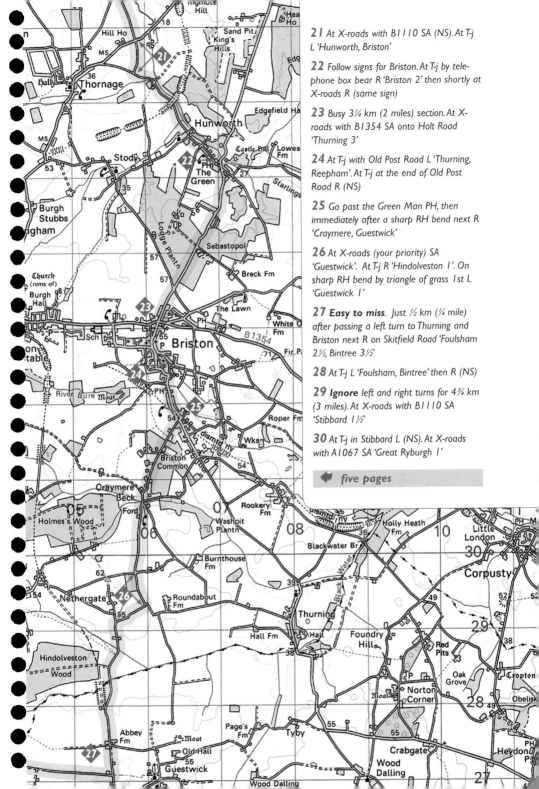

21 At X-roads with B1110 SA (NS). At T-j L 'Hunworth, Briston'

22 Follow signs for Briston. At T-j by telephone box bear R 'Briston 2' then shortly at X-roads R (same sign)

23 Busy 3¼ km (2 miles) section. At X-roads with B1354 SA onto Holt Road 'Thurning 3'

24 At T-j with Old Post Road L 'Thurning, Reepham'. At T-j at the end of Old Post Road R (NS)

25 Go past the Green Man PH, then immediately after a sharp RH bend next R 'Craymere, Guestwick'

26 At X-roads (your priority) SA 'Guestwick'. At T-j R 'Hindolveston 1'. On sharp RH bend by triangle of grass 1st L 'Guestwick 1'

27 **Easy to miss**. Just ½ km (¼ mile) after passing a left turn to Thurning and Briston next R on Skitfield Road 'Foulsham 2½, Bintree 3½'

28 At T-j L 'Foulsham, Bintree' then R (NS)

29 **Ignore** left and right turns for 4¾ km (3 miles). At X-roads with B1110 SA 'Stibbard 1½'

30 At T-j in Stibbard L (NS). At X-roads with A1067 SA 'Great Ryburgh 1'

◀ **five pages**

4 Southwest from Fakenham to Castle Acre

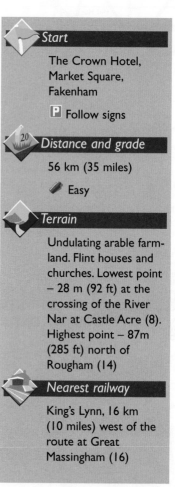

Start

The Crown Hotel, Market Square, Fakenham

P Follow signs

Distance and grade

56 km (35 miles)

Easy

Terrain

Undulating arable farmland. Flint houses and churches. Lowest point – 28 m (92 ft) at the crossing of the River Nar at Castle Acre (8). Highest point – 87m (285 ft) north of Rougham (14)

Nearest railway

King's Lynn, 16 km (10 miles) west of the route at Great Massingham (16)

Castle Acre is one of the most attractive villages in Norfolk: it not only makes a good base for a few days exploring the lanes and tracks in the area, but is also a fine stopping point to aim for half-way round a ride as it has plenty to see, notably the castle and the priory, and several refreshment stops. From Fakenham the ride leaves the valley of the River Wensum, which flows east to the coast at Yarmouth, and after passing through the attractive villages of Whissonsett and Litcham drops into the valley of the River Nar, which flows west into the Great Ouse and thence into The Wash near King's Lynn. After exploring the flint and red-brick delights of Castle Acre the ride turns north through Rougham, passing between hawthorn hedgerows and intensively cultivated fields to arrive at Great Massingham, with its five ponds and wide village green. Carefully avoiding the busy A148 the route threads its way through the Rudhams and Broomsthorpe, rejoins the valley of the River Wensum and passes the pretty round flint church tower in Shereford before returning to the old market square in the heart of Fakenham.

Fakenham   Colkirk   Oxwick   Whissonsett   Tittleshall   Litcham   Great Dunham   Castle Acre

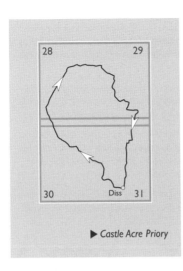

▶ Castle Acre Priory

28   29

30   Diss   31

Refreshments

Lots of choice in **Fakenham**
The Crown PH 🍷🍷, **Colkirk**
Swan Inn, **Whissonsett**
The Bull PH 🍷, **Litcham**
Ostrich PH 🍷🍷, Albert Victor PH,
tearooms, **Castle Acre**
Rose & Crown PH, **Great
Massingham**
Crown PH, Cat & Fiddle PH,
East Rudham

Places of interest

Castle Acre 9
The village is situated on the
ancient Peddars Way and boasts a
huge Norman castle mound and
green, entered through a 13th-
century gate. The remains of the
priory feature fine 12th-century
arcading. There are painted panels
in the 15th-century Church of St
James

Rougham

Great Massingham

East Rudham

Shereford

1 With back to the Crown Hotel in the Market Square, Fakenham, R onto Bridge Street 'Dereham B1146, Swaffham (A1065)'

2 Cross the river. At X-roads (your priority) shortly after the end of the houses in Hempton turn L 'Racecourse. East Dereham B1146'

3 After 1½ km (1 miles) 1st R 'Colkirk'

4 Follow the road through Colkirk. Shortly after the Crown PH 2nd L on Whissonsett Road 'Whissonsett'

5 After 4 km (2½ miles), at T-j by the Swan PH in Whissonsett R 'Raynhams 2½, Tittleshall 3'. Shortly, fork L onto Mill Lane

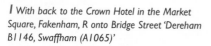 **two pages**

17 After 3¼ km (2 miles), at X-roads in Great Massingham with a large pond to the right turn R 'Harpley 2¼'

18 Towards the end of the village, shortly after the no through road of Mill Lane to the right, next R on Rudham Road 'West Raynham 3¼'

19 After ¾ km (½ mile), with a red brick bungalow to the left, on a sharp RH bend bear L (in effect SA). At X-roads by the Gate House SA (NS). At next X-roads SA (NS)

20 After 3¼ km (2 miles) **ignore** 1st right by telephone box. Take the next R by a triangle of grass with a wooden bench (near to red-brick Hillside Cottages)

21 Shortly before T-j with main road (A148) in East Rudham turn R onto parallel lane with flint and brick wall / railings to your right. At T-j R then 1st L onto Broomsthorpe Road

22 After 2½ km (1½ miles) ignore 1st left. Shortly after passing a large brick and flint house to the left take the next L 'Tatterford 1¼'

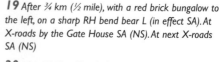

23 At T-j / X-roads SA 'Tatterford, Dunton'.

24 At T-j L 'Dunton, Shereford' then after ½ km (¼ mile) 1st R (NS)

25 At T-j by Give Way sign and triangle of grass R 'Shereford. 2 ton weight limit'. Cross river. At T-j L 'Fakenham 2½'

26 After 3¼ km (2 miles), at X-roads with A1065 SA 'Dereham B1146. Racecourse' then shortly at next X-roads L 'Fakenham Town Centre only' to return to the start

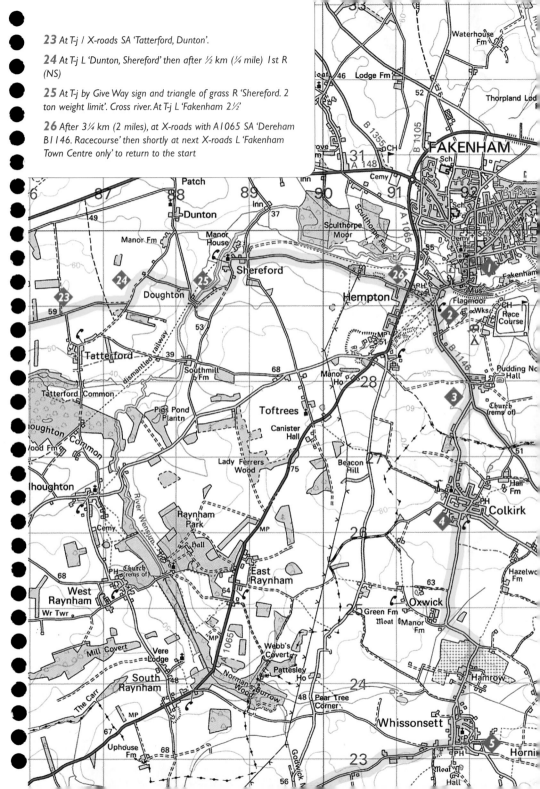

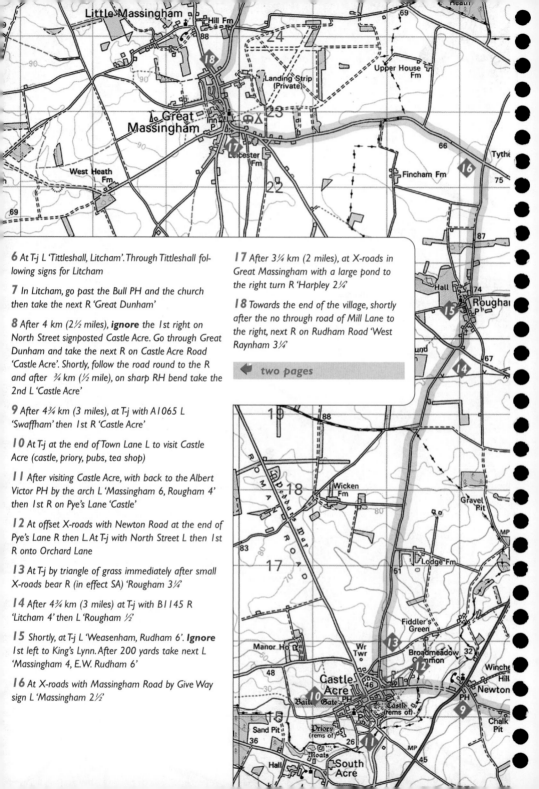

6 At T-j L 'Tittleshall, Litcham'. Through Tittleshall following signs for Litcham

7 In Litcham, go past the Bull PH and the church then take the next R 'Great Dunham'

8 After 4 km (2½ miles), **ignore** the 1st right on North Street signposted Castle Acre. Go through Great Dunham and take the next R on Castle Acre Road 'Castle Acre'. Shortly, follow the road round to the R and after ¾ km (½ mile), on sharp RH bend take the 2nd L 'Castle Acre'

9 After 4¾ km (3 miles), at T-j with A1065 L 'Swaffham' then 1st R 'Castle Acre'

10 At T-j at the end of Town Lane L to visit Castle Acre (castle, priory, pubs, tea shop)

11 After visiting Castle Acre, with back to the Albert Victor PH by the arch L 'Massingham 6, Rougham 4' then 1st R on Pye's Lane 'Castle'

12 At offset X-roads with Newton Road at the end of Pye's Lane R then L. At T-j with North Street L then 1st R onto Orchard Lane

13 At T-j by triangle of grass immediately after small X-roads bear R (in effect SA) 'Rougham 3¼'

14 After 4¾ km (3 miles) at T-j with B1145 R 'Litcham 4' then L 'Rougham ½'

15 Shortly, at T-j L 'Weasenham, Rudham 6'. **Ignore** 1st left to King's Lynn. After 200 yards take next L 'Massingham 4, E.W. Rudham 6'

16 At X-roads with Massingham Road by Give Way sign L 'Massingham 2½'

17 After 3¼ km (2 miles), at X-roads in Great Massingham with a large pond to the right turn R 'Harpley 2¼'

18 Towards the end of the village, shortly after the no through road of Mill Lane to the right, next R on Rudham Road 'West Raynham 3¼'

← **two pages**

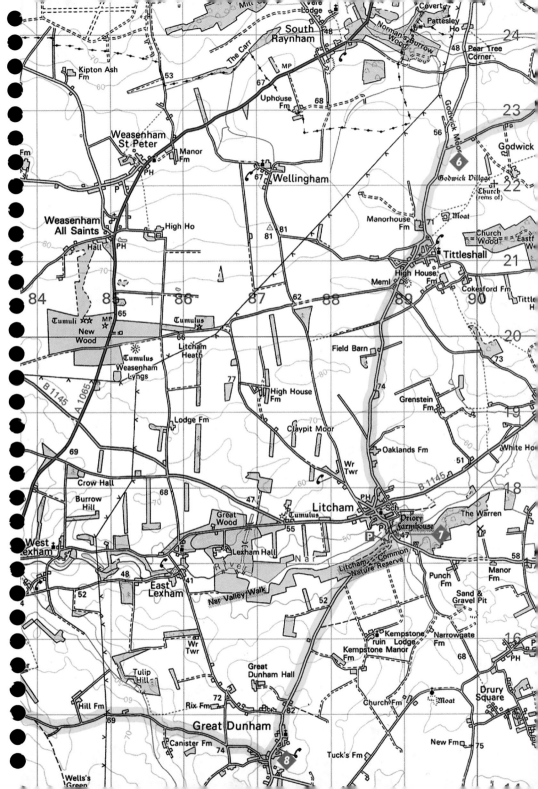

5 North from Aylsham to the coast at Cromer

This on-road ride starts from Aylsham, an attractive town with a fine square and a good base for touring the northeast corner of Norfolk. This part of the region is less intensively cultivated than the land further to the west; there are more fields left to permanent pasture, more trees and woodland and even some common land at Abel Heath to the west of Aylsham, near the start of the ride. The overall impression is nevertheless one of gently rolling arable land dotted with flint churches and occasional attractive old red-brick buildings. Flint is the preferred stone for most of the churches, including the round tower of the church at Bessingham, and sometimes for the bigger houses – note the fine decorated brick and flint window surrounds at Metton Hall and the imposing flint façade of Cromer Hall just to the south of the town. The ride makes its way north to the coast via a maze of quiet lanes then drops over 60 m (200 feet) in the last mile to reach Cromer before climbing up away from the coast to Northrepps and lanes back to Aylsham.

Start

The Post Office / Blackboys Inn, Aylsham, north of Norwich

🅿 Follow signs

Distance and grade

55 km (34 miles)

✎ Easy

Terrain

Undulating arable land, occasional broadleaf woodland, coast. Lowest point – sea level at Cromer. Highest point – 74 m (243 ft) southeast of Cromer

Nearest railway

Cromer

Aylsham Abel Heath Oulton Street Oulton Itteringham Matlaske Bessingham Gresham Metton

Blickling Hall ½ km (1 mile) north of (3)

A Jacobean 17th-century moated hall with an immaculate formal garden and impressive period-style rooms. A huge tapestry hanging in the Peter the Great Room depicts the Russian ruler, and the Long Gallery has an ornate plaster ceiling. There are extensive walks, a crescent-shaped lake, an orangery and a temple in the grounds

Mannington Hall Gardens between 6 and 7

Set around a moated 15th-century house and entered over a drawbridge, the gardens consist of extensive lawns enclosed by yew hedges with statuary busts. There are hundreds of different roses in the Heritage Rose Gardens, a lake with a stone bridge, woodland paths and nature trails

Felbrigg Hall ½ km (1 mile) off the route between 11 and 12

Jacobean home of the Windham family for three centuries, built around 1620. There are furnishings and pictures from the 18th-century, windows with medieval stained glass, elegant rococo plasterwork and a Gothic library. The grounds contain a walled garden, orangery, woodland and lakeside walks

Cromer 13–15

Popular family resort with a sandy beach, the Pavilion Theatre and the Lifeboat Museum. The church tower is the tallest in Norfolk at 48 m (160 ft). A row of Victorian fishermen's cottages forms Cromer Museum, with crabbing industry displays

---

Refreshments:

Greens PH ❦, lots of choice in **Aylsham**
Walpole Arms PH ❦, **Itteringham**
Chequers PH, **Gresham**
Bath House PH ❦, Red Lion PH ❦, lots of choice in **Cromer**
Foundary Arms PH, **Northrepps**
Vernon Arms PH, **Southrepps**

Cromer   Northrepps   Southrepps   Antingham   Tuttington

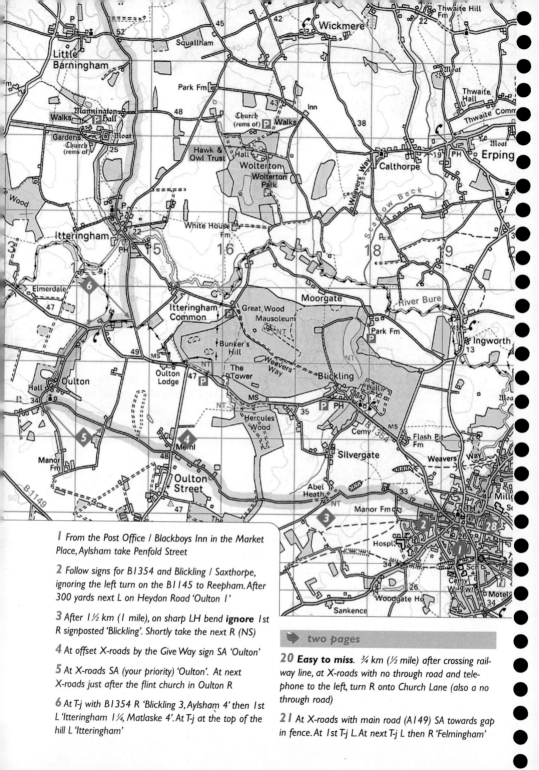

1 From the Post Office / Blackboys Inn in the Market Place, Aylsham take Penfold Street

2 Follow signs for B1354 and Blickling / Saxthorpe, ignoring the left turn on the B1145 to Reepham. After 300 yards next L on Heydon Road 'Oulton 1'

3 After 1½ km (1 mile), on sharp LH bend **ignore** 1st R signposted 'Blickling'. Shortly take the next R (NS)

4 At offset X-roads by the Give Way sign SA 'Oulton'

5 At X-roads SA (your priority) 'Oulton'. At next X-roads just after the flint church in Oulton R

6 At T-j with B1354 R 'Blickling 3, Aylsham 4' then 1st L 'Itteringham 1¼, Matlaske 4'. At T-j at the top of the hill L 'Itteringham'

➡ two pages

20 **Easy to miss**. ¾ km (½ mile) after crossing railway line, at X-roads with no through road and telephone to the left, turn R onto Church Lane (also a no through road)

21 At X-roads with main road (A149) SA towards gap in fence. At 1st T-j L. At next T-j L then R 'Felmingham'

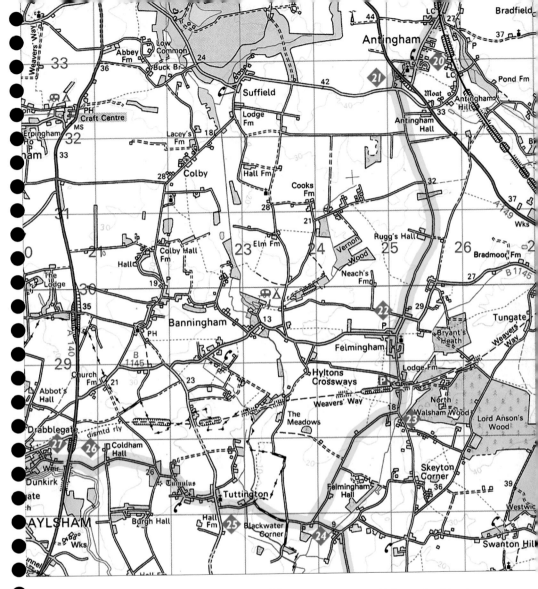

22 *After 4 km (2½ miles) at T-j with B1145 bear R (in effect SA) ie do not turn right to Suffield, then shortly, on sharp RH bend 1st L 'Skeyton 1½, Coltishall 6'*

23 *Shortly after passing beneath railway bridge next R (NS)*

24 *At T-j by triangle of grass R 'Tuttington 1, Banningham 2' [or turn L 'Skeyton 1¼, Westwick 3' for link to on-road route 6 and follow signs for Scottow and Buxton]*

25 *At T-j with Norwich Road R 'Banningham' then L immediately after round-towered flint church*

26 *At X-roads with A140 SA towards wooden gate then lane*

27 *At T-j by round silos L. At T-j at the end of Dunkirk L 'Town Centre'*

28 *At T-j with Red Lion Street at the end of White Hart Street L 'Town Centre' then 1st R to return to the start*

▲ Cromer

14 At next X-roads SA. At T-j with seafront R then 1st L on RH bend '6ft 6ins width limit'

15 At T-j with Church Street L then at traffic lights L onto B1159 'Mundesley'

16 Ignore right turn to hospital. 135 m (150 yards) after the brow of the hill take the 2nd R on Northrepps Road

17 Follow signs for Northrepps for 3¼ km (2 miles) ignoring right and left turns. Shortly after the Foundary Arms PH in Northrepps next R onto Craft Lane 'Southrepps 1½'

18 At T-j by the Vernon Arms PH in Southrepps R 'Thorpe Market 1¼, Roughton 2¾' then 1st L on Long Lane 'Gunton station'

19 At T-j at the end of Chapel Road R 'Railway Station'

7 Follow this road for 6½ km (4 miles), passing through Itteringham and following signs for Matlaske. At X-roads by Give Way sign R 'Matlaske, Aldborough'

8 Through Matlaske past the round-towered church then after sharp RH and LH bend, climb through woodland and take the 1st L 'Bessingham ½, Sheringham 5½'

9 At T-j by church bear L uphill 'Gresham'

10 At X-roads by the round-towered church in Gresham R 'Metton 2¾, Cromer 5¼'

11 Follow signs for Metton through Gresham. ¾ km (½ mile) after the end of the village turn R by triangle of grass and memorial cross 'Metton 1½, Roughton 3½'

12 Follow this road for 5¾ km (3½ miles), passing through Metton. At X-roads (with B1436) by Give Way sign SA

13 After 3¼ km (2 miles) at X-roads at the end of Hall Road in Cromer SA onto Cabbell Road

 two pages

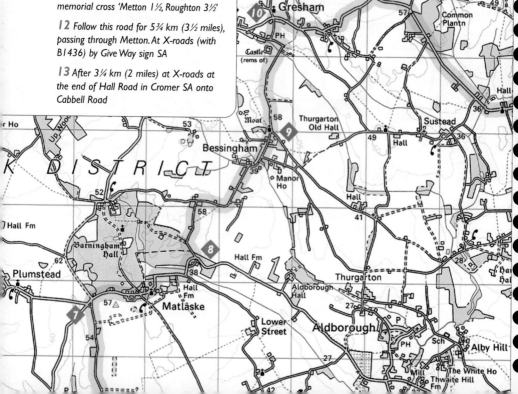

From Aylsham to Wroxham in the heart of the Norfolk Broads

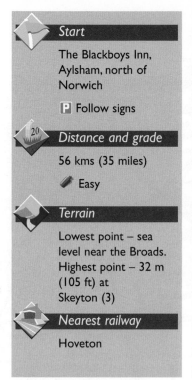

*T*his ride from the attractive town of Aylsham heads southeast towards the Broads and into Wroxham, the busy heart of the boating activity in the region. The land is predominantly arable with some pasture and clumps of broadleaf woodland, although the 'Oak Belt' to the south of Swanton Abbott is more pine than oak. The hedgerows are mainly hawthorn and it is heartening to see that in places more hedges have been planted, reversing a trend of many years which saw fields growing larger and larger with the consequent loss of hedgerows and the wildlife corridors that they provide. The ride passes large, old, thatched red-brick barns near to Sloley Hall on its way east into Broads country at Irstead. In the Broads one has the impression of more woodland, more thatched houses and a slightly more relaxed attitude towards land use. Of architectural note is a delightful thatched flint-and-brick house just south of Irstead and the thatched red-brick church of St Peters just north of Hoveton. Wroxham's role as boating centre can be seen in the flotillas of boats ready for hire at the bridge over the River Bure. It is a bustling town with the busy A1151 passing through it on its way towards Norwich. The course of the River Bure is followed roughly northwest from Wroxham back towards Aylsham, rejoining the outwards route near Burgh.

Aylsham · Burgh next Aylsham · Swanton Abbott · Scottow · Cat's Common · Irstead Street

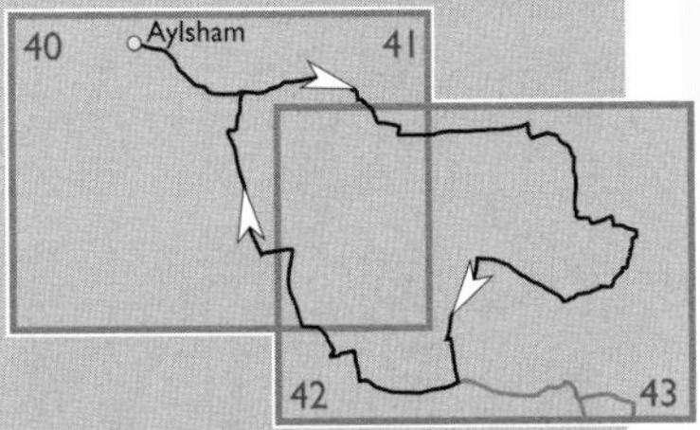

Places of interest

***Aylsham* 1**
A market town with splendid old buildings: the Manor House and Abbots Hall date from the early 1600s and the Old Hall from 1689. The rose-covered grave of the landscape gardener Humphry Repton lies in the churchyard of the 14th-century St Michael's Church

***Bure Valley Railway* 1**
A narrow gauge line runs along the trackbed of the old Great Eastern for 15km (9 miles) beside the River Bure, between Aylsham and Wroxham

▼ *Horning*

Hoveton Wroxham Crostwick Frettenham Buxton White Cross

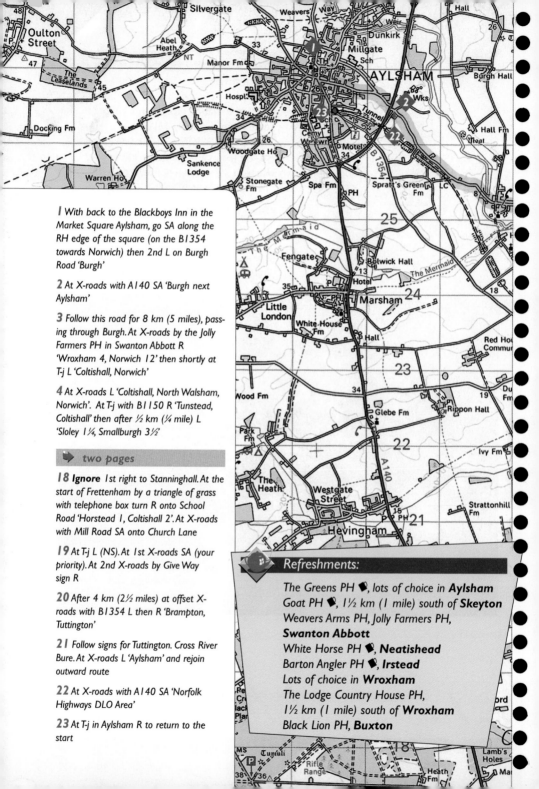

1 With back to the Blackboys Inn in the Market Square Aylsham, go SA along the RH edge of the square (on the B1354 towards Norwich) then 2nd L on Burgh Road 'Burgh'

2 At X-roads with A140 SA 'Burgh next Aylsham'

3 Follow this road for 8 km (5 miles), passing through Burgh. At X-roads by the Jolly Farmers PH in Swanton Abbott R 'Wroxham 4, Norwich 12' then shortly at T-j L 'Coltishall, Norwich'

4 At X-roads L 'Coltishall, North Walsham, Norwich'. At T-j with B1150 R 'Tunstead, Coltishall' then after ½ km (¼ mile) L 'Sloley 1¼, Smallburgh 3½'

➡ **two pages**

18 **Ignore** 1st right to Stanninghall. At the start of Frettenham by a triangle of grass with telephone box turn R onto School Road 'Horstead 1, Coltishall 2'. At X-roads with Mill Road SA onto Church Lane

19 At T-j L (NS). At 1st X-roads SA (your priority). At 2nd X-roads by Give Way sign R

20 After 4 km (2½ miles) at offset X-roads with B1354 L then R 'Brampton, Tuttington'

21 Follow signs for Tuttington. Cross River Bure. At X-roads L 'Aylsham' and rejoin outward route

22 At X-roads with A140 SA 'Norfolk Highways DLO Area'

23 At T-j in Aylsham R to return to the start

Refreshments:

The Greens PH 🍴, lots of choice in **Aylsham**
Goat PH 🍴, 1½ km (1 mile) south of **Skeyton**
Weavers Arms PH, Jolly Farmers PH, **Swanton Abbott**
White Horse PH 🍴, **Neatishead**
Barton Angler PH 🍴, **Irstead**
Lots of choice in **Wroxham**
The Lodge Country House PH, 1½ km (1 mile) south of **Wroxham**
Black Lion PH, **Buxton**

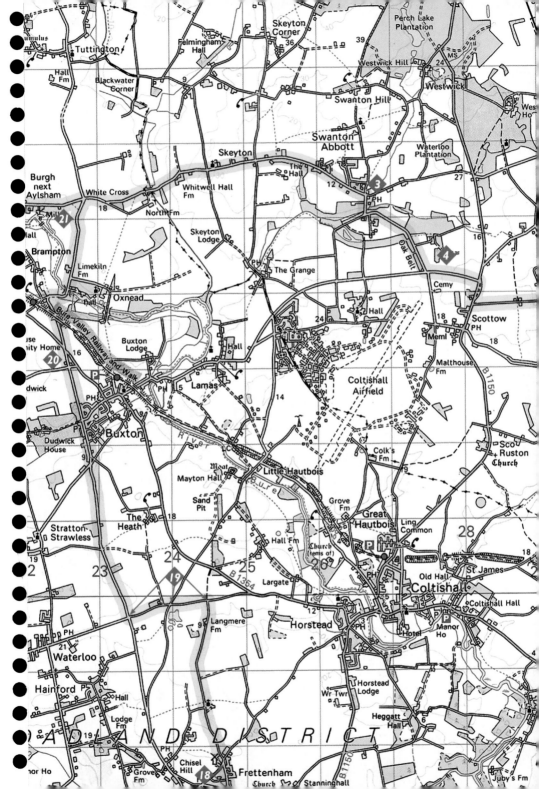

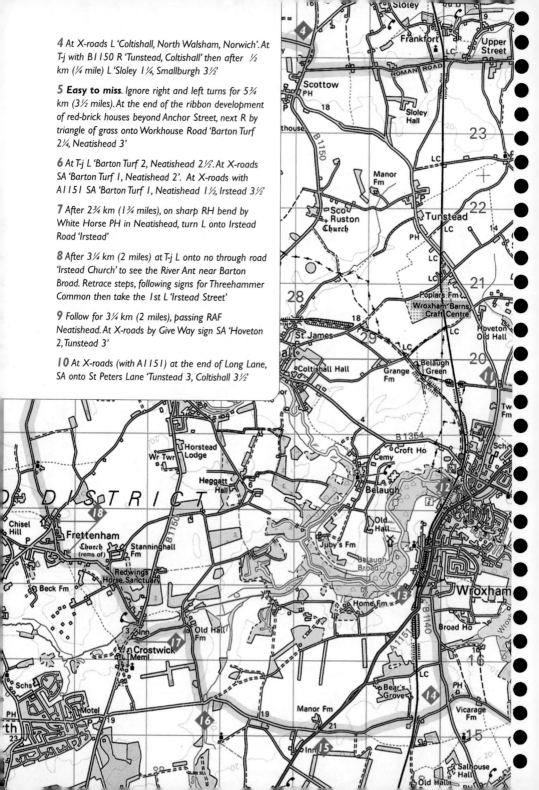

4 At X-roads L 'Coltishall, North Walsham, Norwich'. At T-j with B1150 R 'Tunstead, Coltishall' then after ½ km (¼ mile) L 'Sloley 1¼, Smallburgh 3½'

5 **Easy to miss**. Ignore right and left turns for 5¾ km (3½ miles). At the end of the ribbon development of red-brick houses beyond Anchor Street, next R by triangle of grass onto Workhouse Road 'Barton Turf 2¼, Neatishead 3'

6 At T-j L 'Barton Turf 2, Neatishead 2½'. At X-roads SA 'Barton Turf 1, Neatishead 2'. At X-roads with A1151 SA 'Barton Turf 1, Neatishead 1½, Irstead 3½'

7 After 2¾ km (1¾ miles), on sharp RH bend by White Horse PH in Neatishead, turn L onto Irstead Road 'Irstead'

8 After 3¼ km (2 miles) at T-j L onto no through road 'Irstead Church' to see the River Ant near Barton Broad. Retrace steps, following signs for Threehammer Common then take the 1st L 'Irstead Street'

9 Follow for 3¼ km (2 miles), passing RAF Neatishead. At X-roads by Give Way sign SA 'Hoveton 2, Tunstead 3'

10 At X-roads (with A1151) at the end of Long Lane, SA onto St Peters Lane 'Tunstead 3, Coltishall 3½'

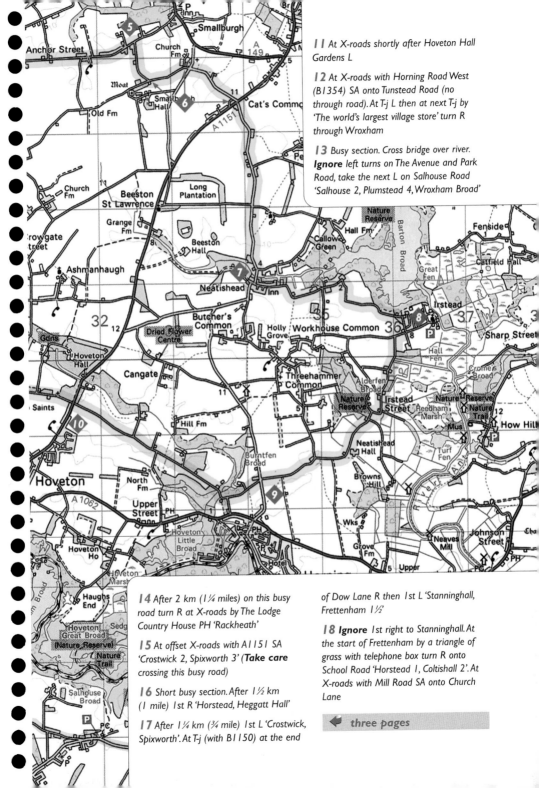

11 At X-roads shortly after Hoveton Hall Gardens L

12 At X-roads with Horning Road West (B1354) SA onto Tunstead Road (no through road). At T-j L then at next T-j by 'The world's largest village store' turn R through Wroxham

13 Busy section. Cross bridge over river. **Ignore** left turns on The Avenue and Park Road, take the next L on Salhouse Road 'Salhouse 2, Plumstead 4, Wroxham Broad'

14 After 2 km (1¼ miles) on this busy road turn R at X-roads by The Lodge Country House PH 'Rackheath'

15 At offset X-roads with A1151 SA 'Crostwick 2, Spixworth 3' (**Take care** crossing this busy road)

16 Short busy section. After 1½ km (1 mile) 1st R 'Horstead, Heggatt Hall'

17 After 1¼ km (¾ mile) 1st L 'Crostwick, Spixworth'. At T-j (with B1150) at the end of Dow Lane R then 1st L 'Stanninghall, Frettenham 1½'

18 **Ignore** 1st right to Stanninghall. At the start of Frettenham by a triangle of grass with telephone box turn R onto School Road 'Horstead 1, Coltishall 2'. At X-roads with Mill Road SA onto Church Lane

◀ three pages

From Swaffham to Cockley Cley, the Nar Valley and Castle Acre

Swaffham has a fine, wide market square in its centre and many attractive old buildings stand around the edge of the square. The town lies on the geological divide between the chalk and flint to the north and the sandier soils of Breckland to the south. Towards Brandon and Thetford the land is good only for forestry plantations of pines, in complete contrast to the richer soils in the rest of East Anglia. The ride heads southwest to Cockley Cley where there is a fascinating recreation of an Iceni village; the Iceni were the tribe led by Queen Boudicca who gave their name to the Icknield Way which runs from the Thames near Goring to the start of the Peddars Way near Thetford. The twisted Scots Pines near Cockley Cley were caused by the original hedges being allowed to grow up due to lack of manpower during World War I. Glimpses of Oxborough Hall can be caught through the iron gates at the western end of the village. The tall lime trees and the slightly decayed, untouched feel about the nature reserve near Oxborough Wood stand in dramatic contrast to the intensive land use all around.

Start

White Hart Inn, Market Square, Swaffham

P Follow signs

Distance and grade

55 kms (34 miles)

Easy

Terrain

Sandy woodland south of Swaffham, open, arable farmland, wooded valley of the River Nar. Lowest point – 3m (10 feet) at the Oxborough Wood Nature Reserve (5). Highest point – 85m (280 feet) between Newton and Sporle (15-16)

Swaffham

Cockley Cley

Gooderstone

Oxborough

Boughton

Fincham

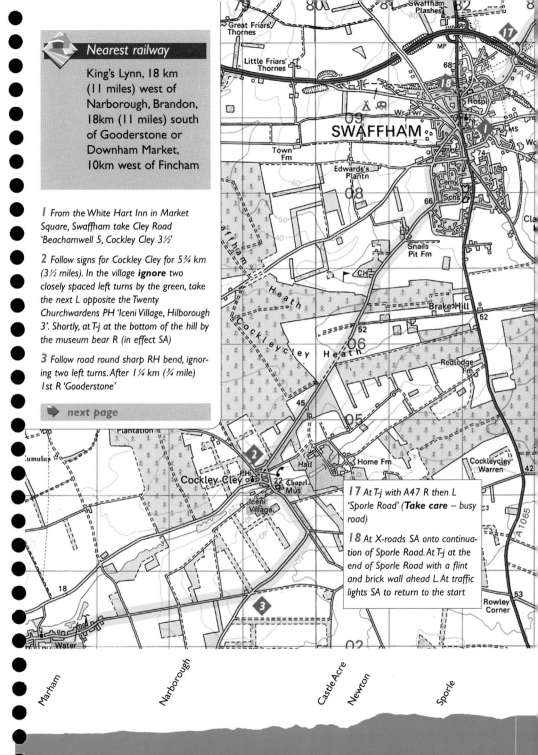

next page

Nearest railway

King's Lynn, 18 km (11 miles) west of Narborough, Brandon, 18km (11 miles) south of Gooderstone or Downham Market, 10km west of Fincham

1 From the White Hart Inn in Market Square, Swaffham take Cley Road 'Beachamwell 5, Cockley Cley 3½'

2 Follow signs for Cockley Cley for 5¾ km (3½ miles). In the village **ignore** two closely spaced left turns by the green, take the next L opposite the Twenty Churchwardens PH 'Iceni Village, Hilborough 3'. Shortly, at T-j at the bottom of the hill by the museum bear R (in effect SA)

3 Follow road round sharp RH bend, ignoring two left turns. After 1¼ km (¾ mile) 1st R 'Gooderstone'

17 At T-j with A47 R then L 'Sporle Road' (**Take care** – busy road)

18 At X-roads SA onto continuation of Sporle Road. At T-j at the end of Sporle Road with a flint and brick wall ahead L. At traffic lights SA to return to the start

4 Through Gooderstone. At X-roads L 'Oxborough'

5 **Easy to miss**. 3¼ km (2 miles) after passing Oxborough Hall, on a sharp LH bend shortly after crossing bridge over stream turn R 'Eastmoor, Beachamwell' then after ¾ km (½ mile) 1st L 'Boughton'

6 At T-j at the end of Oxborough Road bear R onto Chapel Road 'Barton Bendish, Fincham'

7 Through Boughton. 1¼ km (¾ mile) after the village pond 1st L on Gibbet Lane 'Wereham, Fincham' then shortly 1st R on

Fincham Road 'Fincham, Downham Market'

8 At X-roads with the A1122 in Fincham SA onto Marham Road 'Shouldam 2, Marham 2¾'

9 Views! At T-j at the bottom of the hill R 'Marham'

10 The next 9¾ km (6 miles) will have more traffic. Through Marham. After 4 km (2½ miles) at T-j L 'Narborough'

➡ **two pages**

Places of interest

Swaffham 1
The town sign features local benefactor John Chapman, a 15th-century pedlar who found gold coins in his garden and gave money to the parish church. The Market Place is flanked by graceful 18th-century buildings, the Victorian Corn Exchange and old workshops

Cockley Cley 2
Reconstructed encampment of the Iceni tribe at the time of Queen Boudicca, with watch-towers, drawbridge, chariot house and snake pit, on the site of the original. The village contains the remains of a Saxon church

Oxburgh Hall 4-5
A red-brick, moated manor house, built in 1482 by the Bedingfield family, who still live there. There are tapestry panels embroidered by Mary, Queen of Scots, formal French gardens and views from the tower

▼Oxburgh Hall

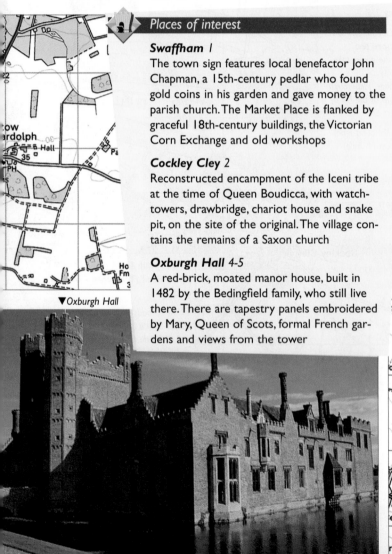

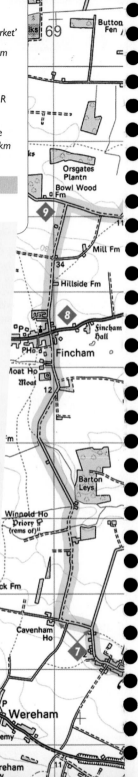

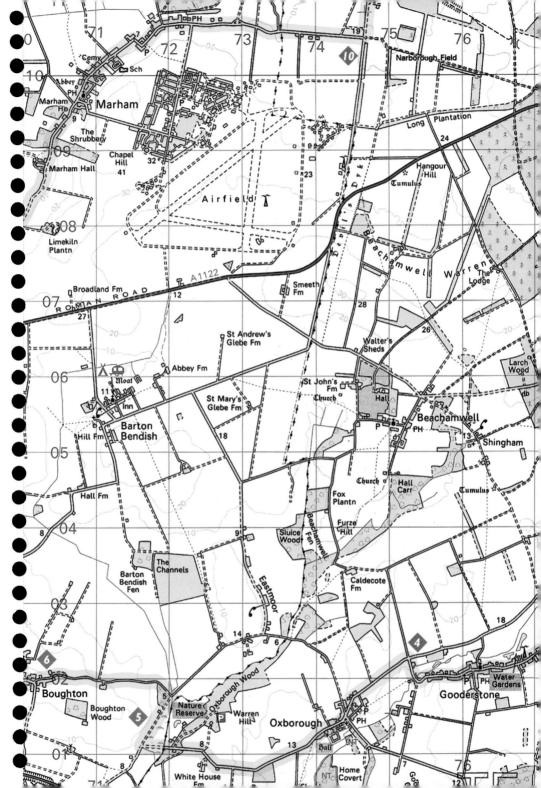

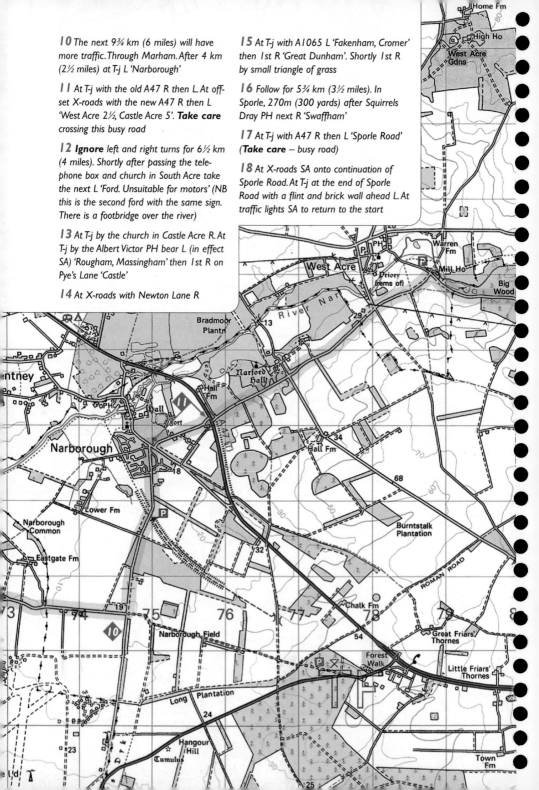

10 The next 9¾ km (6 miles) will have more traffic. Through Marham. After 4 km (2½ miles) at T-j L 'Narborough'

11 At T-j with the old A47 R then L. At off-set X-roads with the new A47 R then L 'West Acre 2½, Castle Acre 5'. **Take care** crossing this busy road

12 **Ignore** left and right turns for 6½ km (4 miles). Shortly after passing the telephone box and church in South Acre take the next L 'Ford. Unsuitable for motors' (NB this is the second ford with the same sign. There is a footbridge over the river)

13 At T-j by the church in Castle Acre R. At T-j by the Albert Victor PH bear L (in effect SA) 'Rougham, Massingham' then 1st R on Pye's Lane 'Castle'

14 At X-roads with Newton Lane R

15 At T-j with A1065 L 'Fakenham, Cromer' then 1st R 'Great Dunham'. Shortly 1st R by small triangle of grass

16 Follow for 5¾ km (3½ miles). In Sporle, 270m (300 yards) after Squirrels Dray PH next R 'Swaffham'

17 At T-j with A47 R then L 'Sporle Road' (**Take care** – busy road)

18 At X-roads SA onto continuation of Sporle Road. At T-j at the end of Sporle Road with a flint and brick wall ahead L. At traffic lights SA to return to the start

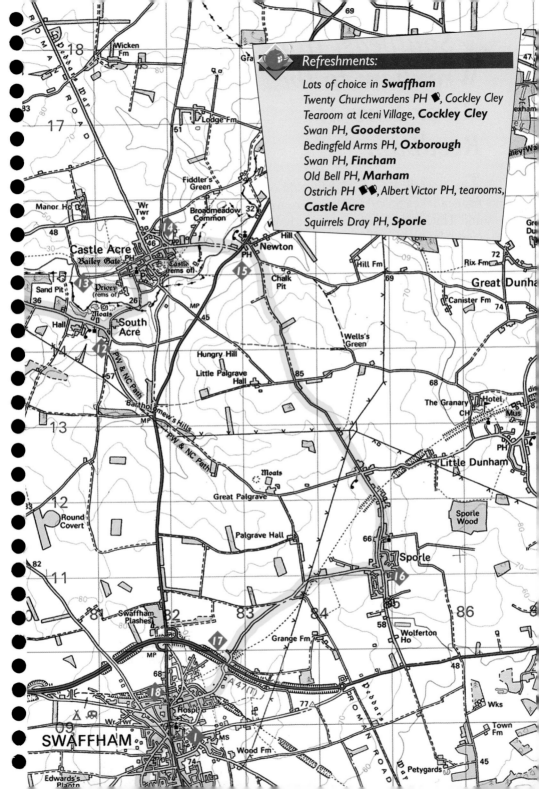

Refreshments:

Lots of choice in **Swaffham**
Twenty Churchwardens PH 🍺, Cockley Cley
Tearoom at Iceni Village, **Cockley Cley**
Swan PH, **Gooderstone**
Bedingfeld Arms PH, **Oxborough**
Swan PH, **Fincham**
Old Bell PH, **Marham**
Ostrich PH 🍺🍺, Albert Victor PH, tearooms,
Castle Acre
Squirrels Dray PH, **Sporle**

Southeast from Wroxham to the River Yare at Reedham

Start

The bridge over the River Bure in Wroxham, 13 km (8 miles) northeast of Norwich

P Follow signs

Distance and grade

60 km (37 miles)

🖊 Easy

Terrain

Into the Broads, reed beds and wetlands betwen Reedham and Blofield. At or close to sea level for most of the ride

The Norfolk Broads, a collection of reed-fringed lakes linked by the rivers Ant, Bure and Thurne, are without doubt best appreciated from a boat. Nevertheless, there are times when the network of lanes comes close to the water's edge, particularly at the Visitor Centre and Nature Trail at Ranworth Broad. Starting from Wroxham, the centre of boating activity in the Broads, the ride is unavoidably on busy roads for the first and last stretches. However, the outlook improves as the route swings east through the pretty, thatched village of Woodbastwick and the watery delights of Ranworth. Acle has little to detain you but Reedham is quite the opposite – it really feels as though it is a last outpost, with marshes and rivers acting as natural barriers on three sides and only a ferry carrying vehicles across the River Yare. There is the famous swing bridge for the railway, which opens to allow the passage of yachts and craft up the River Yare. West from here, careful attention should be paid to the instructions as there are several junctions to be navigated in order to stay as close as possible to the reed beds and the nature reserves near to the River Yare. Large conurbations, such as Norwich, have a habit of generating lots of traffic on all the roads within a few miles radius of the centre, even on minor roads, hence the meandering course through Panxworth to rejoin the outward route at Woodbastwick.

Wroxham   Woodbastwick   Ranworth   South Walsham   Upton   Acle   Moulton St. Mary

Hoveton (Wroxham),
Acle or Reedham

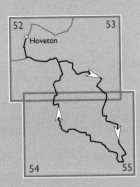

Ranworth 5

A steep climb to the top of St Helen's Church tower is rewarded with by vast Broadland views. The glorious 15th-century rood screen is painted with saints, apostles and martyrs

Ranworth Broad 5

There is a boardwalk nature trail through woodland and marshland to the floating Broadland Conservation Centre, which has displays explaining the history and wildlife of Norfolk Broads, with a bird-watching gallery upstairs

Reedham 15

A nautical village! The chain ferry over the River Yare is the only crossing for 42 km (26 miles) between Norwich and Great Yarmouth. The flint-walled church stands aloof on a ridge behind the village. There are exotic birds at the nearby Animal Park

Strumpshaw Fen 22

Typical fenland country beside the River Yare, with reed and sedge beds, woodland, marshes and meadows rich in birdlife which can be seen from a net-work of foopaths and hides. The Steam Museum has engines and a small railway

Refreshments:

Lots of choice in **Wroxham**
Fur & Feather PH ♥♥, **Woodbastwick**
Maltsters PH, Granary Restaurant, **Ranworth**
The Ship PH ♥, **South Walsham**
Kings Head PH, **Acle**
Ship PH, Lord Nelson PH, Railway Tavern PH ♥, tearooms, **Reedham**
Kings Head PH, **Blofield**

edham   Limpenhoe   Buckenham   Blofield   Panxworth   Woodbastwick

▼ Ranworth Broad

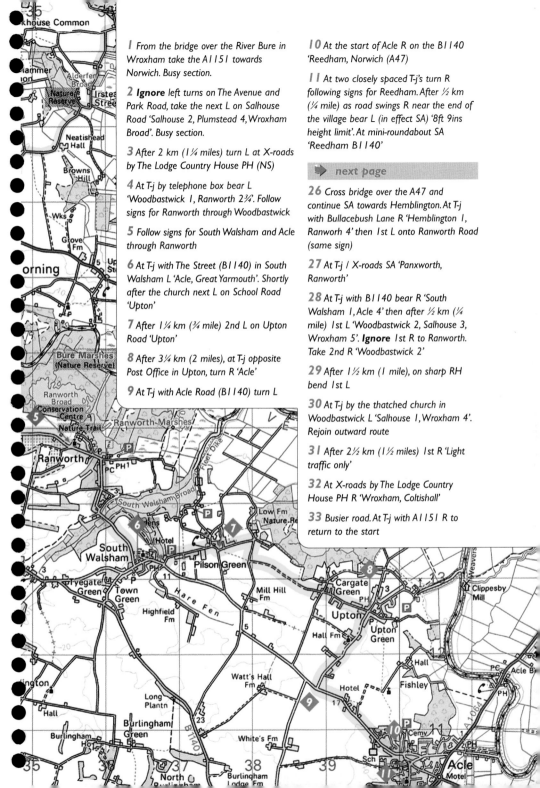

1 From the bridge over the River Bure in Wroxham take the A1151 towards Norwich. Busy section.

2 *Ignore* left turns on The Avenue and Park Road, take the next L on Salhouse Road 'Salhouse 2, Plumstead 4, Wroxham Broad'. Busy section.

3 After 2 km (1¼ miles) turn L at X-roads by The Lodge Country House PH (NS)

4 At T-j by telephone box bear L 'Woodbastwick 1, Ranworth 2¾'. Follow signs for Ranworth through Woodbastwick

5 Follow signs for South Walsham and Acle through Ranworth

6 At T-j with The Street (B1140) in South Walsham L 'Acle, Great Yarmouth'. Shortly after the church next L on School Road 'Upton'

7 After 1¼ km (¾ mile) 2nd L on Upton Road 'Upton'

8 After 3¼ km (2 miles), at T-j opposite Post Office in Upton, turn R 'Acle'

9 At T-j with Acle Road (B1140) turn L

10 At the start of Acle R on the B1140 'Reedham, Norwich (A47)

11 At two closely spaced T-j's turn R following signs for Reedham. After ½ km (¼ mile) as road swings R near the end of the village bear L (in effect SA) '8ft 9ins height limit'. At mini-roundabout SA 'Reedham B1140'

26 Cross bridge over the A47 and continue SA towards Hemblington. At T-j with Bullacebush Lane R 'Hemblington 1, Ranworh 4' then 1st L onto Ranworth Road (same sign)

27 At T-j / X-roads SA 'Panxworth, Ranworth'

28 At T-j with B1140 bear R 'South Walsham 1, Acle 4' then after ½ km (¼ mile) 1st L 'Woodbastwick 2, Salhouse 3, Wroxham 5'. *Ignore* 1st R to Ranworth. Take 2nd R 'Woodbastwick 2'

29 After 1½ km (1 mile), on sharp RH bend 1st L

30 At T-j by the thatched church in Woodbastwick L 'Salhouse 1, Wroxham 4'. Rejoin outward route

31 After 2½ km (1½ miles) 1st R 'Light traffic only'

32 At X-roads by The Lodge Country House PH R 'Wroxham, Coltishall'

33 Busier road. At T-j with A1151 R to return to the start

11 At two closely spaced T-j's turn R following signs for Reedham. After ½ km (¼ mile) as road swings R near the end of the village bear L (in effect SA) '8ft 9ins height limit'. At mini-roundabout SA 'Reedham B1140'

12 Easy to miss. After 4¾ km (3 miles) 1st proper L onto Halvergate Road 'Halvergate 1¼, Great Yarmouth'

13 At T-j at the end of Moulton Road R 'Freethorpe' then shortly, on sharp RH bend, bear L

14 After 5¾ km (3½ miles), by the car park for Animal Adventure Park, turn R on Church Road 'Reedham Village Centre' then after ¾ km (½ mile) 1st L (same sign)

15 Follow the road through Reedham. At T-j with Station Road by the memorial stone L. At T-j by the railway station R 'Freethorpe'

16 Ignore 1st left on Station Drive. After ¾ km (½ mile) next L 'Limpenhoe 1'

17 At junction by farm R then L onto Reedham Road 'Limpenhoe'

18 At T-j by triangle of grass with a five-windowed house ahead turn R then shortly at next T-j at the end of Reedham Road L towards the church

19 After the church, follow the road around to the R then 1st L onto Cantley Road 'Cantley'

20 At X-roads SA 'Lingwood'. **Easy to miss.** Follow the road round to the R then after ¾ km (½ mile), immediately after a large thatched, red-brick barn on the left take the next L (NS)

21 At T-j by letter box L (NS). After ¾ km (½ mile) 1st L onto no through road 'Buckenham Railway Staion'. Cross railway line and turn R

22 Shortly after the next railway crossing 1st L (NS) opposite thatched red-brick barns

23 At T-j at the end of Low Road L. Shortly, at next T-j R then L (NS)

24 At T-j by triangle of grass after crossing bridge over the railway L then R (NS)

25 At T-j after the church in Blofield R 'Woodbastwick, Wroxham'. At traffic lights at X-roads with the old A47 SA (same sign)

26 Cross bridge over the A47 and continue SA towards Hemblington. At T-j with Bullacebush Lane R 'Hemblington 1, Ranworth 4' then 1st L onto Ranworth Road (same sign)

◄ previous page

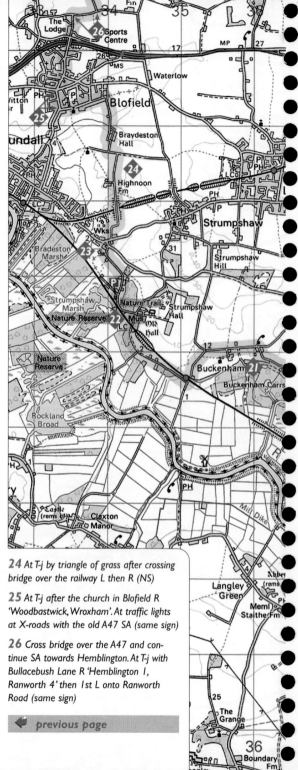

9 *Along the Yare valley from Norwich to Loddon*

Norwich has a fairly enlightened attitude towards cycling, and to the northwest of the city there is an excellent track known as the Marriotts Way which has been created from a dismantled railway starting near the city centre and running for several miles to Reepham. To the southeast of Norwich there are two much shorter sections of dedicated cyclepath which help you out of the city and over the A47, avoiding main roads. There are lovely views of the River Yare near to Kirby Bedon complete with pleasure boats and anglers. This is followed by what must be one of the steepest hills in Norfolk! There are many attractive old red-brick barns and buildings, some with thatched roofs. Try not to miss the ruins of the castle and the manor house at Claxton. Down on the marshes, cattle graze during the summer months. The tidal creek at Hardley Flood on the River Chet just beyond Langley Street reminds you how far inland the sea affects the water levels. There is an unusual thatched tower on the church in Chedgrave and many fine old buildings of brick and flint around the handsome square in Loddon. On the return route to Norwich, every attempt is made to avoid the busier lanes and roads that draw traffic into the region's capital.

 Start

Bonds Shopping Centre in Norwich

P If arriving by car, it is better to park at (3) at the bottom of Long John Hill, starting and finishing the ride here

 Distance and grade

51 km (32 miles)

Easy

 Terrain

River valley, reed beds, gently undulating arable land. Lowest point – sea level at several points along the Waveney valley. Highest point – 65m (213 ft) at Upper Stoke (22)

Norwich   Trowse Newton   Bramerton   Surlingham   Rockland St Mary   Langley Green   Langley Street

Nearest railway

Norwich

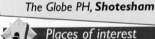

58   59

Norwich

Chedgrave

60   61

▶ Norwich Cathedral

Refreshments:

Lots of choice in **Norwich**
Woods End Tavern, **Woods End**
New Inn, **Rockland**
Beauchamp Arms PH, near **Claxton**
The Wherry PH, **Langley Green**
White Horse PH, **Chedgrave**
Swan PH ◥, Angel PH, Fox & Hounds
PH, **Loddon**
The Globe PH, **Shotesham**

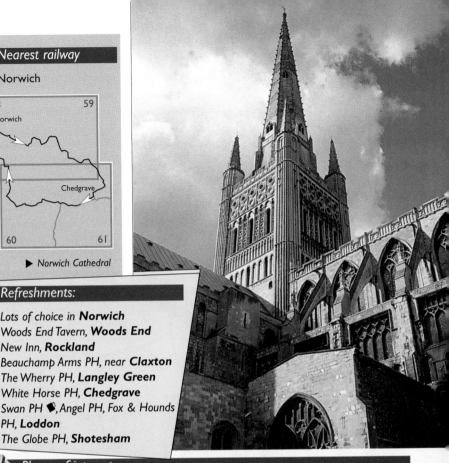

Places of interest

Norwich I

East Anglia's flourishing capital has one of the country's most beautiful cathedrals, started in 1094. The nave roof and cloisters have bosses painted with Biblical scenes and grotesque creatures. The city centre has some 30 medieval churches and is dominated by Norwich Castle which houses a military museum. There are death masks of executed prisoners in the dungeons. Museums abound: there are archaeology and art galleries in the castle; the medieval Stranger's Hall has period rooms depicting domestic life from Tudor to Victorian times

Chedgrave
Loddon   Mundham   Seething   Kirstead Hall   Shotesham   Upper Stoke

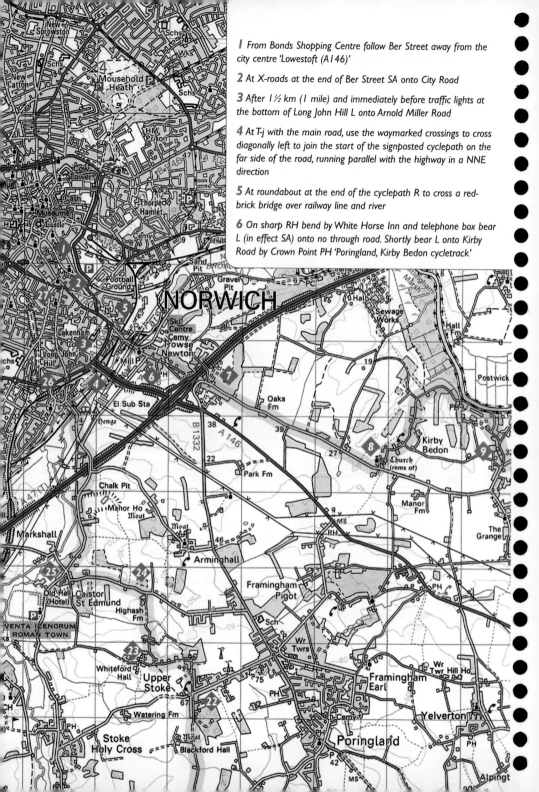

1 From Bonds Shopping Centre follow Ber Street away from the city centre 'Lowestoft (A146)'

2 At X-roads at the end of Ber Street SA onto City Road

3 After 1½ km (1 mile) and immediately before traffic lights at the bottom of Long John Hill L onto Arnold Miller Road

4 At T-j with the main road, use the waymarked crossings to cross diagonally left to join the start of the signposted cyclepath on the far side of the road, running parallel with the highway in a NNE direction

5 At roundabout at the end of the cyclepath R to cross a red-brick bridge over railway line and river

6 On sharp RH bend by White Horse Inn and telephone box bear L (in effect SA) onto no through road. Shortly bear L onto Kirby Road by Crown Point PH 'Poringland, Kirby Bedon cycletrack'

7 Follow signs for Kirby Bedon. Cross bridge over A47. At T-j L 'Kirby Bedon'

8 After 4 km (2½ miles), having ignored left turn to water treatment works, 1st proper L onto The Street 'Wood End 1'

9 Follow the lane alongside river, climb steeply, at T-j by triangle of grass L 'Surlingham 1½'

10 Into Surlingham. Towards the end of the village turn R by triangle of grass onto Mill Road 'Rockland 1½, Claxton 3'

11 At T-j at the end of Surlingham Lane L 'Claxton 1½, Langley 3¾'

12 After 6½ km (4 miles), on sharp RH bend by memorial cross and The Wherry PH, bear L (in effect SA) onto Langley Street 'Langley Street ½, Hardley 2'

 next page

22 After 4 km (2½ miles), at X-roads by Give Way sign and telephone box in Upper Stoke SA 'Caistor St Edmund, Trowse'

23 Go round sharp LH bend then after ¾ km (½ mile) 1st R 'Valley Farm Lane. 7.5 ton weight limit'

24 At T-j at the end of High Ash Lane L (NS)

25 At X-roads by Give Way sign R 'Arninghall'

26 Busier section. Cross the A47. At traffic lights SA onto Long John Hill to rejoin outward route

27 At X-roads with Bracondale at the end of City Road SA onto Ber Street to return to the start

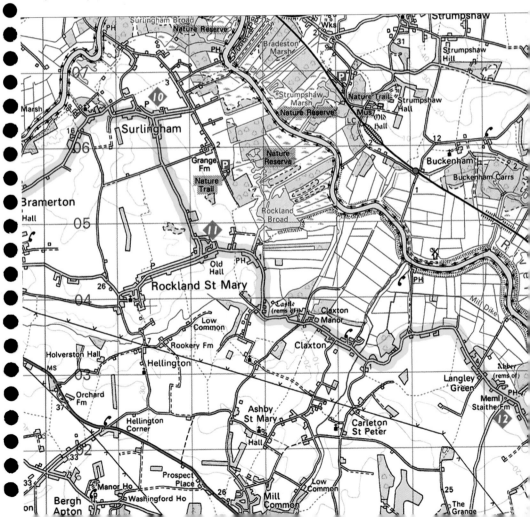

12 After 6½ km (4 miles), on sharp RH bend by memorial cross and The Wherry PH, bear L (in effect SA) onto Langley Street 'Langley Street ½, Hardley 2'

13 At T-j with Cross Stone Road by small red-brick bus shelter turn R 'Carleton St Peter 2½, Loddon 1¾'

14 After ¾ km (½ mile) at the next T-j R 'Loddon 1¼, Chedgrave 1'

15 At X-roads at the end of Hardley Road L 'Loddon ¼. At T-j by White Horse PH in Chedgrave turn L

16 Cross bridge then 1st R just past Kings Head PH in Loddon 'Seething 3½, Brooke 5½'

17 At offset X-roads with A146 R then L 'Mundham 2¼, Sisland ½'

18 Through Mundham and Seething. **Easy to miss.** 3¼ km (2 miles) after Seething Church L onto Church Road by the square-towered flint church at Kirstead

19 After ½ km (¼ mile), on sharp LH bend (Zig Zag Lane) turn R 'Brooke 1¼'. At X-roads (with B1332) by Give Way sign SA onto Littlebeck Lane

20 At T-j at the end of Mill Lane R 'Brooke 1½, Shotesham 1½' then shortly, at T-j with High Green L 'Shotesham 1½'

21 Easy to miss. ¾ km (½ mile) after the 'Shotesham' sign at the start of the village, next R onto Chapel Lane 'Poringland 2½'. After ¾ km

(½ mile), on sharp RH bend bear L (in effect SA) 'Stoke Holy Cross 2'

22 After 4 km (2½ miles), at X-roads by Give Way sign and telephone box in Upper Stoke SA 'Caistor St Edmund, Trowse'

23 Go round sharp LH bend then after ¾ km (½ mile) 1st R 'Valley Farm Lane. 7.5 ton weight limit'

← two pages

10 North from Diss to Attleborough

*T*his ride starts from Diss, an old town lying on the boundary between Norfolk and Suffolk. The boundary at this point, as along so much of its length, is formed by the River Waveney. Throughout East Anglia there are signs of airfields that were built during the Second World War and used by Allied planes in their attacks on German positions. East Anglia was an ideal location: flat, close to the European mainland and out of reach of the V1 and V2 bombs that were directed at London towards the end of the war. This ride passes close to three such airfields. As the demand for aggregate for the construction of motorways has increased, many of the airfields have been dug up for their stone and concrete. The ride crosses flat arable land towards the attractive village of Kenninghall with its fine brick and flint walls and pargetting on Church Farm House, a decorative feature frequently seen in Suffolk and Essex. A little further on, Quidenham's delights include a Viking mound, an unusual round and octagonal church tower, an ornate lodge house to Quidenham Park, and a tea shop at the Post Office. Attleborough's charms are restricted to the small area around the green. A few miles southeast of the town, just south of Carleton Rode, you will come across the extraordinary fairy tale thatch at Fen Farm. The ride turns south and heads across the fertile landscape back to Diss.

Start

The Museum in the Market Place, Diss, just off the A143 between Bury St Edmunds and Lowestoft

P Follow signs

Distance and grade

48 km (30 miles)

Easy

Terrain

Undulating arable land. Lowest point – 25m (82 ft) at Quidenham. Highest point – 72m (236 ft) near Carleton Rode

Refreshments:

Lots of choice in **Diss**
Tea shop at PO, **Quidenham**
White Lodge PH, lots of choice in **Attleborough**

Diss — Bressingham — Kenninghall — Eccles Road — Attleborough

Diss or Attleborough

28	29
30	Diss 31

▼ Bressingham Gardens

Diss 1

The town has twisting streets with Tudor, Georgian and Victorian architecture and is busy on Friday market days. The imposing Church of St Mary's dates from the 12th century. The 2½ ha (6 acre) mere is a haven for wildfowl

Bressingham Gardens 1½ km
(1 mile) south of the route at 4

An extensive 210 ha (500 acre) nursery makes an unusual setting for the steam locomotive collection. There are more than 5000 varieties of alpines, heathers, conifers and perennials. The narrow-gauge railway runs across the valley of the River Waveney. There is a splendid Victorian steam roundabout in the museum

Flaxlands Hargate Tibenham Heywood Hall

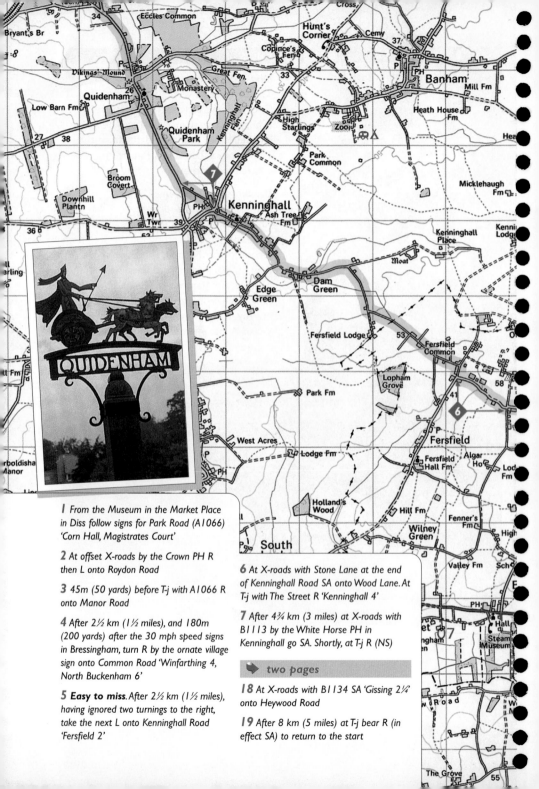

1 From the Museum in the Market Place in Diss follow signs for Park Road (A1066) 'Corn Hall, Magistrates Court'

2 At offset X-roads by the Crown PH R then L onto Roydon Road

3 45m (50 yards) before T-j with A1066 R onto Manor Road

4 After 2½ km (1½ miles), and 180m (200 yards) after the 30 mph speed signs in Bressingham, turn R by the ornate village sign onto Common Road 'Winfarthing 4, North Buckenham 6'

5 Easy to miss. After 2½ km (1½ miles), having ignored two turnings to the right, take the next L onto Kenninghall Road 'Fersfield 2'

6 At X-roads with Stone Lane at the end of Kenninghall Road SA onto Wood Lane. At T-j with The Street R 'Kenninghall 4'

7 After 4¾ km (3 miles) at X-roads with B1113 by the White Horse PH in Kenninghall go SA. Shortly, at T-j R (NS)

➡ **two pages**

18 At X-roads with B1134 SA 'Gissing 2¼ onto Heywood Road

19 After 8 km (5 miles) at T-j bear R (in effect SA) to return to the start

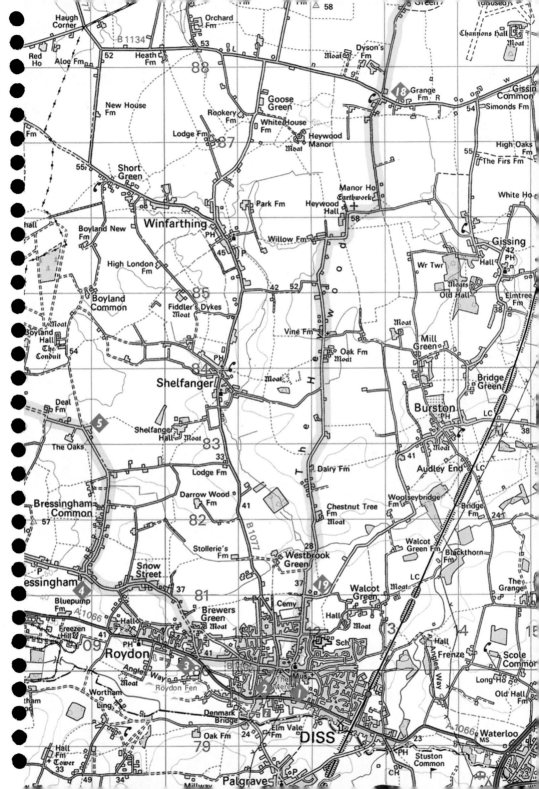

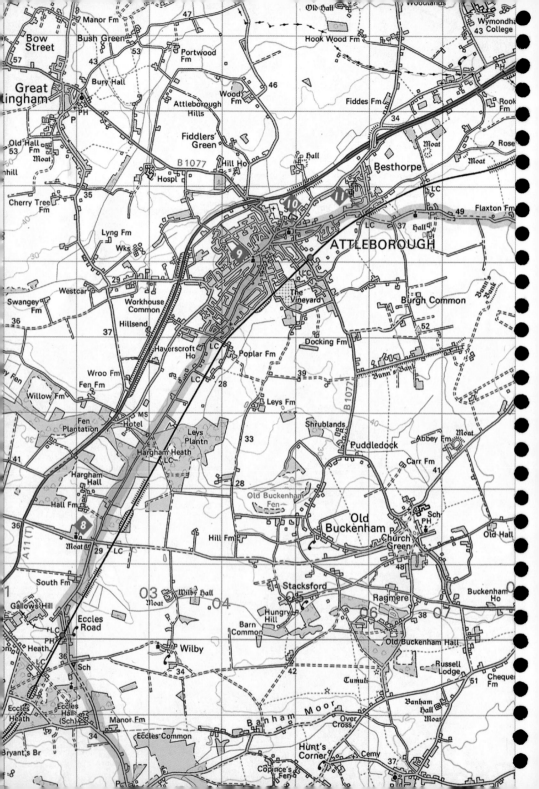

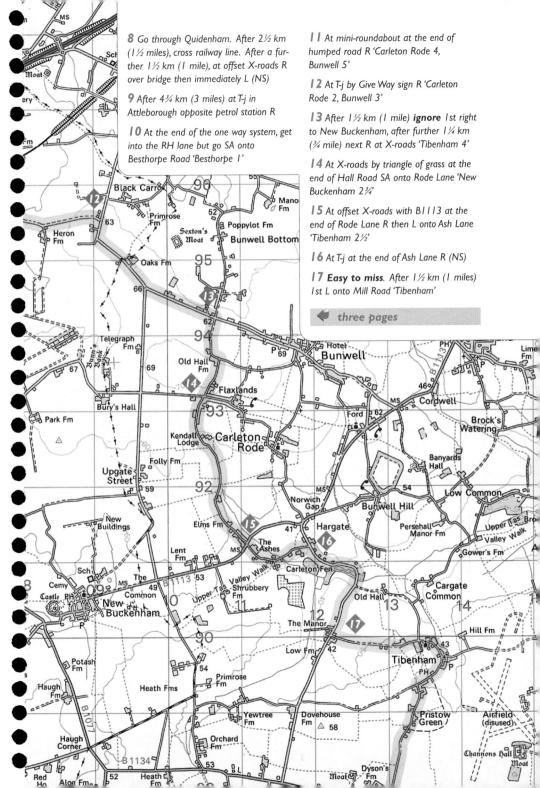

8 Go through Quidenham. After 2½ km (1½ miles), cross railway line. After a further 1½ km (1 mile), at offset X-roads R over bridge then immediately L (NS)

9 After 4¾ km (3 miles) at T-j in Attleborough opposite petrol station R

10 At the end of the one way system, get into the RH lane but go SA onto Besthorpe Road 'Besthorpe 1'

11 At mini-roundabout at the end of humped road R 'Carleton Rode 4, Bunwell 5'

12 At T-j by Give Way sign R 'Carleton Rode 2, Bunwell 3'

13 After 1½ km (1 mile) **ignore** 1st right to New Buckenham, after further 1¼ km (¾ mile) next R at X-roads 'Tibenham 4'

14 At X-roads by triangle of grass at the end of Hall Road SA onto Rode Lane 'New Buckenham 2¾'

15 At offset X-roads with B1113 at the end of Rode Lane R then L onto Ash Lane 'Tibenham 2½'

16 At T-j at the end of Ash Lane R (NS)

17 **Easy to miss**. After 1½ km (1 miles) 1st L onto Mill Road 'Tibenham'

three pages

Southeast from Beccles to the coast at Southwold

Start

St Michael's Church tower in the centre of Beccles, 17 miles southeast of Norwich

P Free parking near Tourist Information Centre, follow signs

Distance and grade

51 km (32 miles)

Easy

Terrain

Arable land with some broadleaf woodland between Beccles and the coast. Crumbling coastline at Covehithe. Lowest point – sea level at Southwold. Highest point – 36m (118 ft) between Brampton railway station and Beccles

This ride explores Suffolk rather than Norfolk or Cambridgeshire. The attractive town of Beccles has one of the most confusing one-way systems in the region, hence the amount of instruction needed to guide you out of town to the start of the curiously named Cucumber Lane and into the heart of the Suffolk countryside. On its way southeast to the coast, the ride runs through gently undulating arable land. There are occasional pockets of permanent pasture and woodland, with trees particularly in evidence around the estate of Sotterley Hall. You will pass flint churches and red-brick houses and barns, normally with red tiles but occasionally thatched. Covehithe has two outstanding curiosities: a road which is gradually retreating before the onslaught of the sea, and a small thatched church built within the ruins of a much larger church. The last 3-5 kilometres (2–3 miles) of the ride into Southwold are busy and unavoidable. The charms of this seaside town and its many fine taverns should be recompense for the unwelcome volume of traffic – if you can, avoid fine weekends in the summer when the roads are likely to be at their busiest. On your return journey to Beccles, keep an eye out for the intricate stonework on the church at Stoven.

Beccles   Ellough   Wrentham   Covehithe   South Cove   Cove Bottom

Nearest railway

Beccles

70	71
Beccles	
72	Southwold 73

▼ Southwold

Places of interest

Beccles 1

Mellow old town on the River Waveney with handsome red-brick Georgian houses. The best-preserved are in Ballygate and Northgate. Gardens run down to the waterside, which is fringed with boat-houses

Southwold 16

Once a Saxon fishing port and now a charming seaside town. Set around nine greens, there are period houses and Dutch-gabled cottages, many painted in pinks and pale blues. The white-washed 1890 lighthouse can be seen from all over town. A ship's figurehead stands outside Park Lane Cottage; there are more in the Sailors' Reading Room in East Street. The Perpendicular Church of St Edmund houses 'Southwold Jack', a 15th-century mechanical figure of an armoured foot soldier. When a cord is pulled, his battleaxe strikes a bell

Refreshments:

Lots of choice in **Beccles**
Crown PH 🍴🍴, lots of choice in **Southwold**
Angel PH 🍴🍴, **Wangford**
Cherry Tree PH, **Stoven**
Dog Inn 🍴, **Brampton**

Southwold   Reydon   Wangford   Stoven   Brampton   Brampton Station   Ringsfield Corner

1 From the T-j near St Michael's church-tower in the centre of Beccles, follow signs for Ipswich and Lowestoft, bearing L along Market Street and SA at two sets of traffic lights

2 At mini-roundabout at the end of Station Road by railway station turn R onto Gosford Road

3 Cross railway line. At T-j at the end of Grove Road, L then 1st R onto B1127 (Ellough Road) 'Hulver' and immediately R again onto Castle Hill

4 Take the 3rd L onto Coney Hill then 1st R onto Banham Road

5 Once again, 3rd L onto Oak Lane then immediately R onto Cucumber Lane

6 At T-j at the end of Cucumber Lane L. After 1¼ km (¾ mile) 1st R at X-roads 'Sotterley 1¾, Southwold 9'

7 At T-j by triangle of grass with oak tree turn R 'Sotterley ¾, Wangford 4½'

8 After 1½ km (1 mile) L at X-roads by memorial cross 'Wrentham 3½, Henstead 2½'

9 At T-j with telephone box ahead R 'Wrentham 2½, Southwold 6¾'. After 1¼ km (¾ mile) follow road round sharp LH bend

10 At X-roads by church and large, attractive thatched house SA 'Wrentham B1127' then 1st L onto Priory Road

11 At X-roads (with A12) SA onto lane opposite. After ½ km (¼ mile) 1st R (NS) opposite thatched wooden barns to the left then at T-j L (NS)

➡ next page

22 After 3¼ km (2 miles) cross the railway line. At T-j 1¼ km (¾ mile) after the railway crossing R 'Ringsfield 3, Beccles 4½'

23 **Ignore** left and right turnings for 6½ km (4 miles). At X-roads at the end of Ringsfield Road on the outskirts of Beccles SA onto Ballygate 'Town Centre' and follow back to the start

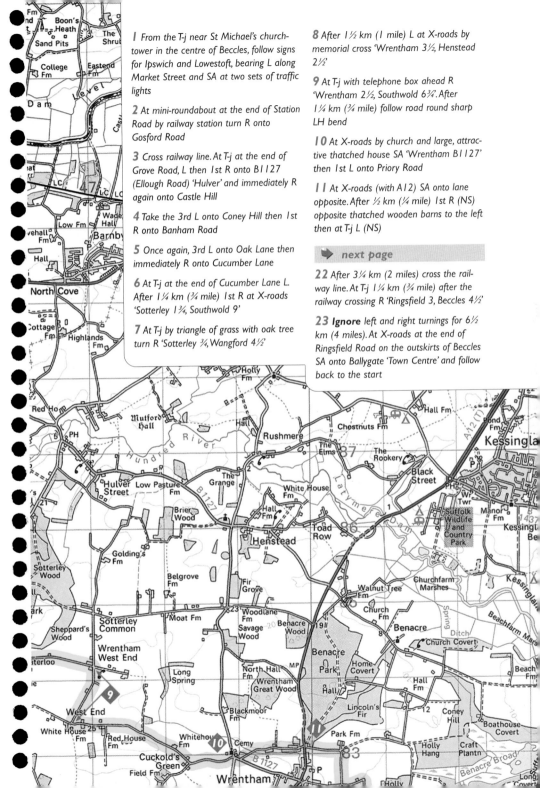

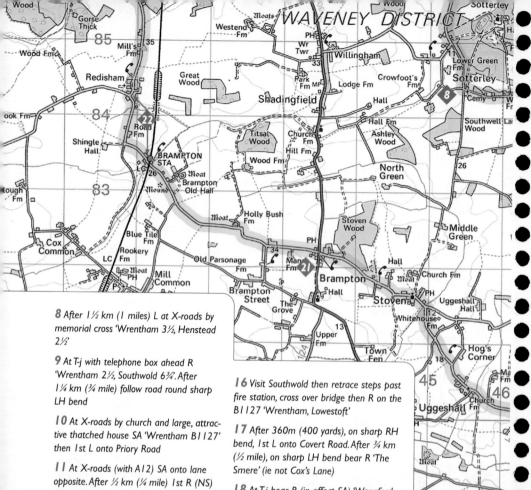

8 After 1½ km (1 miles) L at X-roads by memorial cross 'Wrentham 3½, Henstead 2½'

9 At T-j with telephone box ahead R 'Wrentham 2½, Southwold 6¾'. After 1¼ km (¾ mile) follow road round sharp LH bend

10 At X-roads by church and large, attractive thatched house SA 'Wrentham B1127' then 1st L onto Priory Road

11 At X-roads (with A12) SA onto lane opposite. After ½ km (¼ mile) 1st R (NS) opposite thatched wooden barns to the left then at T-j L (NS)

12 Beyond the church in Covehithe, go SA through 'No pedestrian access' to the end of the road to see the sea. Retrace steps then 1st L shortly after the church 'Southwold 5'

13 At T-j with B1127 L 'Southwold 3½'. **Ignore** 1st right opposite flint and thatch church. Shortly take the next R 'Cove Bottom ½'. **Take care** – this is a right turn on a blind bend; go past the turning, cross the road when you can see both ways then return

14 At T-j (with B1127) R (NS)

15 Busy 3¼ km (2 miles) section into Southwold. At T-j with A1095 L 'Southwold'

16 Visit Southwold then retrace steps past fire station, cross over bridge then R on the B1127 'Wrentham, Lowestoft'

17 After 360m (400 yards), on sharp RH bend, 1st L onto Covert Road. After ¾ km (½ mile), on sharp LH bend bear R 'The Smere' (ie not Cox's Lane)

18 At T-j bear R (in effect SA) 'Wangford 2¾'

19 At T-j R 'Wangford ¾'. At T-j at the end of Wood Farm Lane L 'Wangford ¾'

20 At X-roads (with B1126) at the end of Elms Lane turn R then at X-roads with A12 SA 'Stoven, Uggeshall'

21 Follow signs for Stoven and Brampton for 5½ km (3½ miles). At X-roads with A145 by the Dog Inn SA onto Station Road 'Brampton Station 2½, Bungay 9½'

22 After 3¼ km (2 miles) cross the railway line. At T-j 1¼ km (¾ mile) after the railway crossing R 'Ringsfield 3, Beccles 4½'

← *previous page*

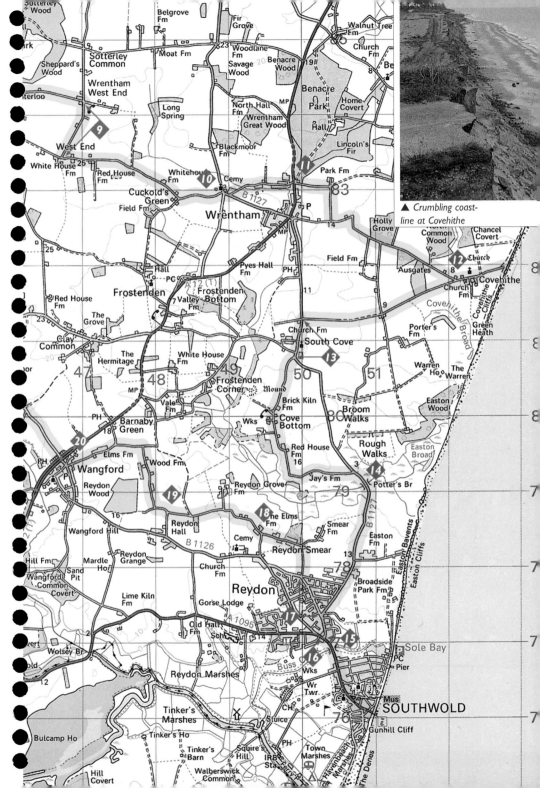

▲ Crumbling coast-
line at Covehithe

West from Framlingham via quiet Suffolk lanes to the attractive village of Debenham

This ride starts from Framlingham, deep in the heart of Suffolk. The route takes you past many attractive thatched cottages and pretty villages, almost all of which boast flint-built churches and an ornate village sign that depicts one of the most salient characteristics of the locale. The country-side is gently undulating with many wild flowers growing in the verges besides the road. The antique centre in Debenham is a fine, ornate building and the village has other attractive half-timbered and thatched properties. One of the best attractions of the ride is at the end – the working windmill at Saxtead Green.

Start

The Square, Framlingham, 24 km (15 miles) northeast of Ipswich

P Follow signs for long-stay car park on Albert Road, just off the B1116 road to Wickham Market

Distance and grade

46 km (29 miles)

Easy

Terrain

No major hills. Lowest point – 24 m (80 ft) in Framlingham. Highest point – 64 m (210 ft) near to Worlingworth

Nearest railway

Wickham Market, 10 km (6 miles) south-east of Framlingham

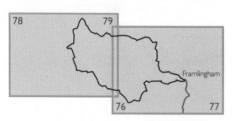

Framlingham

Earl Soham

Broad Green

▼ Morris dancers at Saxtead Green

Framlingham 1
Market town with a patchwork of architectural periods dating from the 12th century. The castle, dating from 1100, was largely rebuilt in the 16th century and has a walk linking nine of the towers, two ditches and the lower court beside the artificial lake. The church contains splendid 16th-century Howard monuments

Earl Soham 2
The church contains some superb woodwork: a double hammerbeam roof spans the nave, and the bench-ends are carved with a rich variety of birds, beasts, angels and men. The nearby rectory dates from Tudor times

Saxtead Green 15
Superb example of an 18th-century Suffolk post mill in full working order, with three-storey roundhouse, sails and fantail

Otley Hall (just off the route) 16
Fine panelling and Jacobean wall decorations are outstanding features of this 16th-century house. Magnificent gardens

Helmingham Hall (just off the route) 16
Tudor house with moated gardens, herbaceous borders and rare roses

Refreshments

Plenty of choice **in Framlingham**
Victoria PH 🍺🍺, Falcon PH 🍺, **Earl Soham**
The Bell PH 🍺🍺, **Cretingham** (just off the route)
Cherry Tree PH, Red Lion PH 🍺, The Angel PH, **Debenham**
Black Horse PH 🍺, **Thorndon** (just off the route)
Beaconsfield Arms PH, **Occold**
Plough Inn PH, **Southolt** The Swan PH, **Worlingworth**

Thorndon   Bedingfield   Worlingworth   Tannington   Saxtead Green

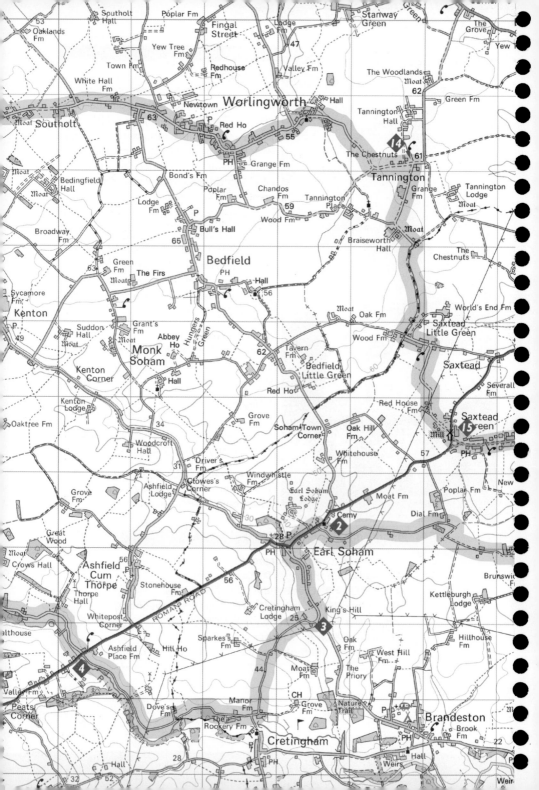

1 With back to the Crown PH in the square in Framlingham, head downhill towards the painted Framlingham sign. At T-j (with B1116) L, then after 300 m (yd), just past the Railway Inn on your left, R on to Brook Lane

2 Follow this lane, ignoring left and right turns, for 5½ km (3½ miles). At T-j with main road (A1120) by the church L, then shortly after The Falcon PH L by the telephone box 'Brandeston 2, Wickham Market 7'

3 After 1½ km (1 mile) on sharp LH bend R by triangle of grass (NS)

4 Continue on this lane for 5 km (3 miles), following signs for Debenham. At X-roads with A1120 SA 'Debenham'

➡ **next page**

13 At X-roads in Bedingfield L 'Worlingworth 3½, Stradbroke 5', then 1st R at X-roads after 800 m (½ mile) 'Southolt 1, Worlingworth 2'

14 Through Southolt and Worlingworth. 1½ km (1 mile) after Worlingworth at T-j by telephone box R 'Saxstead 2½, Framlingham 5'

15 At offset X-roads with A1120 R then L 'Framlingham 2, Saxmundham 9'

16 At T-j with B1116 in Framlingham R 'Framlingham Castle'. On sharp RH bend after 400 m (¼ mile) by the White Horse PH, bear L on to Bridge Street 'Market Hill'.

5 At T-j (with B1077) after 3 km (2 miles) R 'Aspall 2, Eye 8'

6 Just past the Red Lion PH in Debenham L, then bear R 'Unsuitable for HGV'. Ignore left and right turns, continue SA on to Little London Hill 'Wetheringsett 3, Mendlesham 6'

7 After 3 km (2 miles), on sharp LH bend with a pink house ahead, R by triangle of grass 'Thorndon 4, Eye 8'

8 After 5 km (3 miles) at slightly offset X-roads by a triangle of grass R (signs for every other direction except this one!)

9 At T-j by church in Thorndon R 'Debenham 5, Framlingham 13' (or left for the Black Horse PH)

10 At T-j with B1077 L 'Eye 3, Norwich 26, Occold 1'

11 After 1½ km (1 mile) on sharp LH bend 2nd R 'Occold, Bedingfield 2'

12 After 3 km (2 miles), just after a sharp RH bend, 1st L 'Bedingfield 1, Monk Soham 4'

◄ previous page

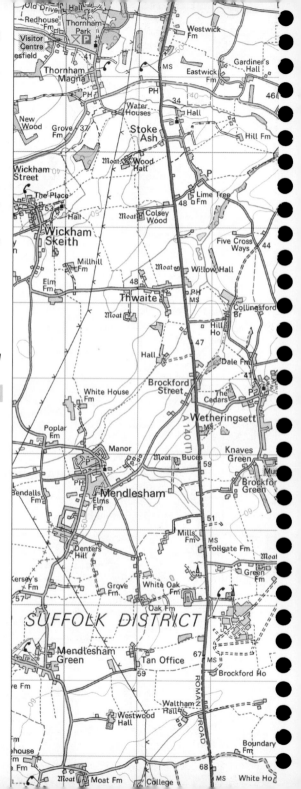

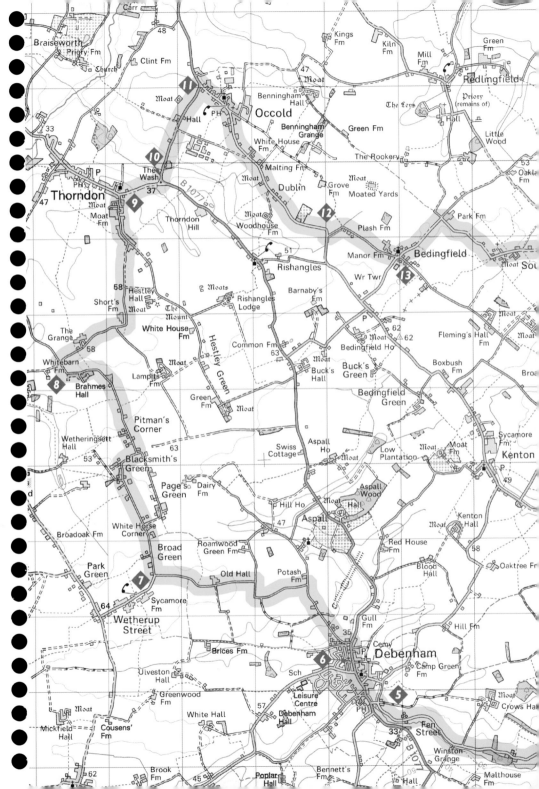

13 The marshlands of the River Waveney northeast of Bungay

Start

Kings Hotel in the heart of Bungay, 25 km (15 miles) southeast of Norwich

P Follow signs

Distance and grade

55 km (34 miles)

✎ Easy

Terrain

Arable farmland, reed beds, attractive flint village of Loddon. Lowest point – sea level at various points on the River Waveney. Highest point – 43 m (141 ft) just north of Hedenham

This ride explores the triangle of land lying between the Rivers Yare and Waveney. It starts by heading southwest from the attractive town of Bungay, and you may wish to visit the Otter Trust, which lies less than a mile off the route beyond Earsham, at the start of the ride. The imposing façade of Earsham Hall is the first of several fine houses passed along the course of the route; the next is at the crossroads with the B1332 near the Mermaid PH south of Hedenham. Flint churches punctuate a gently undulating countryside dedicated to arable farming and occasional broadleaf woodland. Loddon has a fine square at its heart, with an ornate flint library standing on one side and further handsome red-brick buildings clustered close to the centre of the village. The flint church at Heckingham has a hexagonal tower with thatch. Beyond here the ride passes east into the marshland that lies to the north and south of the River Waveney. The ride then heads back west towards Bungay along lanes just to the north of the River Waveney which, for much of its length, forms the boundary between Norfolk and Suffolk.

▶ *Spink's Hill church, north of Ditchingham*

Bungay Earsham Hedenham Seething Mundham Loddon Heckingham Thurlton Lower Thurlton

Nearest railway

Beccles, 3 km (2 miles) south of the route at 16 / 17 or Haddiscoe Station, 3 km (2 miles) north of the route at 11

Places of interest

Bungay *1*

The village is dominated by the stone towers of the 12th-century castle gatehouse and the pinnacle of the 12th-century church of St Mary, part of a Benedictine nunnery whose ruined walls are visible in the churchyard. The elegant 18th-century houses were built after a fire in 1688

Bungay Otter Trust *(near 1)*

The otters are in near-natural surroundings beside the River Waveney at Earsham and have been bred to protect the species from extinction. There are woods, lakes with abundant waterfowl, a night heronry and a nature trail

Raveningham Gardens *3km (2 miles) south of the route at 7-8*

There are rare plants, shrubs and trees in the gardens surrounding the elegant Georgian house

Refreshments:

Green Dragon PH ☙, lots of choice in **Bungay**
Mermaid PH, **Hedenham**
Swan PH ☙, Angel PH, Fox & Hounds PH, **Loddon**
Queens Head PH, **Thurlton**
Crown Inn ☙, **Haddiscoe**
Waveney Inn, **Staithe**

Haddiscoe   Staithe   Boon's Heath   Aldeby   A143   A146   Hungry Hill   Ditchingham

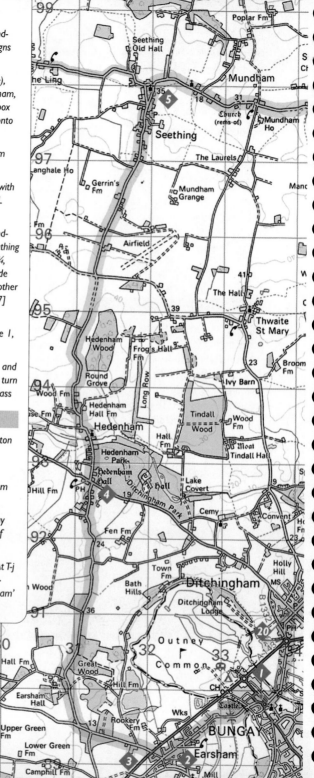

1 *From the Kings Hotel near the round-about in the heart of Bungay follow signs for Earsham along the Earsham Road*

2 Easy to miss. *After 1½ km (1 mile), towards the end of the village of Earsham, 180m (200 yards) after a telephone box on the left, turn R by memorial cross onto no through road by Queens Head PH*

3 *At X-roads with A143 SA 'Hedenham 3¼, Bedingham, Topcroft'*

4 *After 4¾ km (3 miles), at X-roads (with B1332) at the end of Earsham Road L then R onto Church Road*

5 *After 6½ km (4 miles), at T-j by round-towered, flint and thatch church in Seething turn R onto Loddon Road 'Mundham ¾, Loddon 2¾ [***Or** for link to Norwich ride turn L 'Kirstead 1½, Brooke 2', do the other ride and rejoin this ride at instruction 7]*

6 *After 4 km (2½ miles), at offset X-roads with A146 R then L 'Chedgrave 1, Loddon ¼'*

7 *At T-j in Loddon R. Go past Angel PH and Fox & Hounds PH. On sharp RH bend turn L onto Norton Road by a triangle of grass*

◀ two pages

17 *At X-roads (with B1140) SA 'Stockton ½, Kirby Cane 2¾'*

18 *At X-roads (with A146) SA onto Bungay Road 'Ditchingham 3, Hedenham 4'*

19 *Follow signs for Broome and Bungay for 4¾ km (3 miles). At T-j at the end of Bungay Road bear L (in effect SA)*

20 *At X-roads SA onto Loddon Road. At T-j with B1332 L 'Bungay 1' then at round-about 2nd exit 'Wainford Mill, Mettingham' to return to the start*

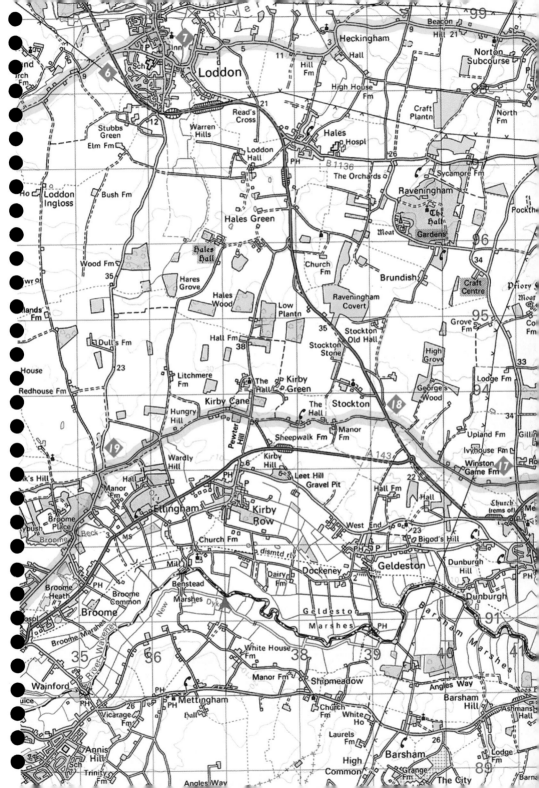

8 After 5¾ km (3½ miles) at T-j with B1140 in Thurlton bear R (in effect SA) 'Gillingham 4¾, Haddiscoe 2¼'

9 Shortly, cross bridge then on sharp RH bend by the Queens Head PH in Thurlton bear L (in effect SA) then 1st L 'Lower Thurlton 1, Marshes'

10 After 3¼ km (2 miles), at T-j by round-towered church L 'Haddiscoe'

11 At T-j (with A143) by the Crown Inn in Haddiscoe R then 1st L onto Wiggs Road 'Aldeby 2½, Burgh St Peter 3'

12 Easy to miss. After 3¼ km (2 miles), shortly after a sharp RH bend 1st L 'Waveney River Centre, Burgh St Peter 2, Staithe'

13 After 4 km (2½ miles), follow the road round to the R by the Waveney Inn. **Ignore** the 1st left on Dick's Mount. Take the next L on Grays Road 'Marshes'

14 At T-j by Give Way sign at the end of Grays Road L

15 After 3¼ km (2 miles), at T-j by thatched bus shelter L 'Beccles 4' then shortly at next T-j L (same sign)

16 At T-j with A143 L 'Diss, Beccles', then after 1¼ km (¾ mile) 1st R by triangle of grass (NS)

17 At X-roads (with B1140) SA 'Stockton ½, Kirby Cane 2¾'

18 At X-roads (with A146) SA onto Bungay Road 'Ditchingham 3, Hedenham 4'

two pages

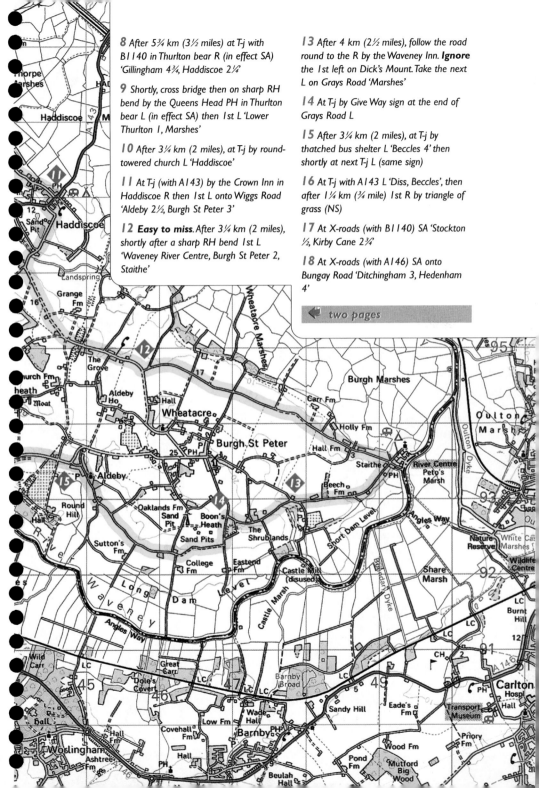

A ring around Hadleigh returning via the attractive villages of Bildeston and Chelsworth

Hadleigh is an attractive, bustling town in south Suffolk. The ride starts southwards following the River Brett before cutting east and northeast on tiny lanes across open farmland towards Washbrook.

The short busy section on the A1071 comes as something of a shock but you are soon back in the domain of the cyclist as attractive lanes bear you north through Flowton and Offton, around the airfield at Wattisham and back via the charms of Bildeston, Chelsworth and Kersey.

Start

The Kings Head PH, the High Street, Hadleigh, 16 km (10 miles) west of Ipswich

P Long-stay car park just off the High Street near the Kings Head PH

Distance and grade

52 km (33 miles)
Easy / moderate

Terrain

Several climbs of between 15 and 30 m (50 and 100 ft). Lowest point – 10 m (36 ft) at Shelley. Highest point – 88 m (290 ft) at Wattisham

Nearest railway

Manningtree, 11 km (7 miles) southeast of the route at Raydon or Stowmarket, 10 km (6 miles) north of the route at Ringshall

Hadleigh   Lower Layham   Great Wenham   Burstall   Flowton

Hadleigh 1
Town of colour-washed houses with decorative plaster work on the walls (pargeting). Fine Georgian and medieval buildings, including a 15th-century Guildhall

▲ *Near Hadleigh*

East Bergholt *(just off the route)* 3
In the heart of Constable country, this is still an unspoilt village. The painter was born here in 1776 in a house near the parish church. Only an outbuilding remains – since converted into a private dwelling

Bildeston 16
Medieval wool centre with multi-coloured Tudor houses. Ghostly footsteps at The Crown, said to be a haunted pub

Chelsworth 17
Timbered cottages, 14th-century church and 18th-century double humped bridge straddling the River Brett

Refreshments

Queens Head PH, **Lower Layham**
Limeburners PH, **Offton**
Red Lion PH, Kings Head PH, Crown PH ❦,
Bildeston
Peacock Inn PH ❦❦, **Chelsworth**
Red Rose PH ❦, **Lindsey Tye**
The Bell PH ❦❦, **Kersey**

Offten Wattisham Chelsworth Kersey

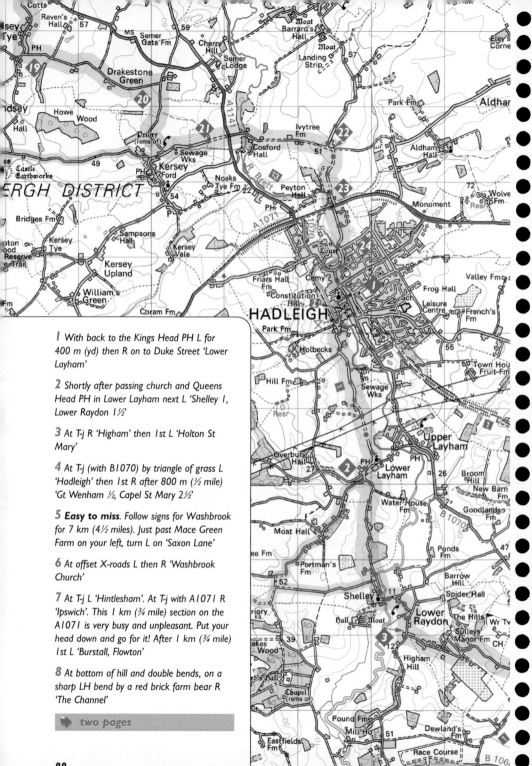

1 With back to the Kings Head PH L for 400 m (yd) then R on to Duke Street 'Lower Layham'

2 Shortly after passing church and Queens Head PH in Lower Layham next L 'Shelley 1, Lower Raydon 1½'

3 At T-j R 'Higham' then 1st L 'Holton St Mary'

4 At T-j (with B1070) by triangle of grass L 'Hadleigh' then 1st R after 800 m (½ mile) 'Gt Wenham ½, Capel St Mary 2½'

5 Easy to miss. Follow signs for Washbrook for 7 km (4½ miles). Just past Mace Green Farm on your left, turn L on 'Saxon Lane'

6 At offset X-roads L then R 'Washbrook Church'

7 At T-j L 'Hintlesham'. At T-j with A1071 R 'Ipswich'. This 1 km (¾ mile) section on the A1071 is very busy and unpleasant. Put your head down and go for it! After 1 km (¾ mile) 1st L 'Burstall, Flowton'

8 At bottom of hill and double bends, on a sharp LH bend by a red brick farm bear R 'The Channel'

➡️ *two pages*

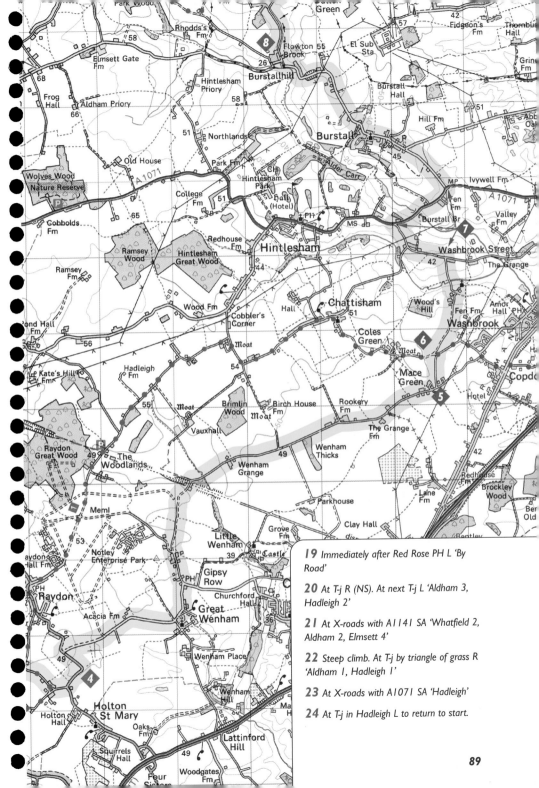

19 Immediately after Red Rose PH L 'By Road'

20 At T-j R (NS). At next T-j L 'Aldham 3, Hadleigh 2'

21 At X-roads with A1141 SA 'Whatfield 2, Aldham 2, Elmsett 4'

22 Steep climb. At T-j by triangle of grass R 'Aldham 1, Hadleigh 1'

23 At X-roads with A1071 SA 'Hadleigh'

24 At T-j in Hadleigh L to return to start.

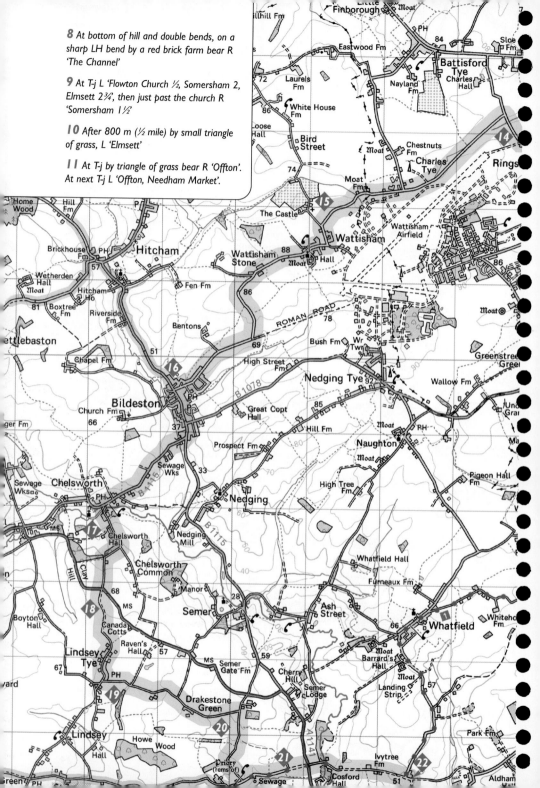

8 At bottom of hill and double bends, on a sharp LH bend by a red brick farm bear R 'The Channel'

9 At T-j L 'Flowton Church ½, Somersham 2, Elmsett 2¾', then just past the church R 'Somersham 1½'

10 After 800 m (½ mile) by small triangle of grass, L 'Elmsett'

11 At T-j by triangle of grass bear R 'Offton'. At next T-j L 'Offton, Needham Market'.

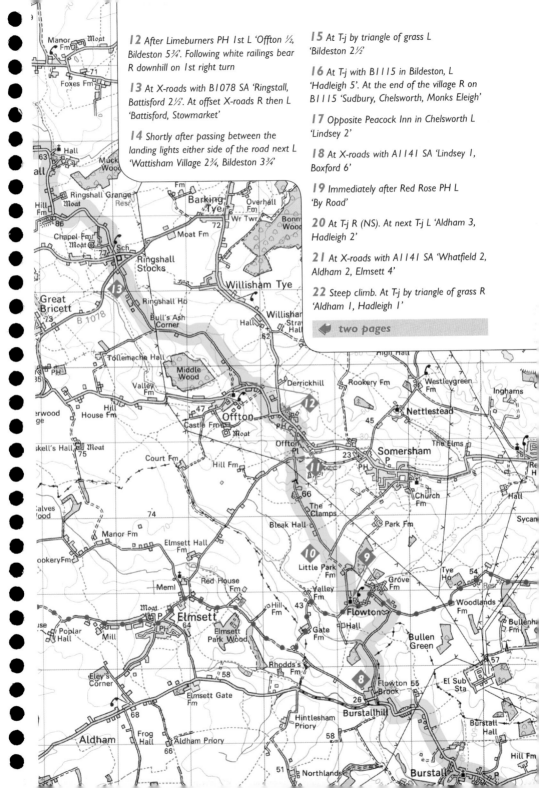

12 After Limeburners PH 1st L 'Offton ½, Bildeston 5¾. Following white railings bear R downhill on 1st right turn

13 At X-roads with B1078 SA 'Ringstall, Battisford 2½'. At offset X-roads R then L 'Battisford, Stowmarket'

14 Shortly after passing between the landing lights either side of the road next L 'Wattisham Village 2¾, Bildeston 3¾'

15 At T-j by triangle of grass L 'Bildeston 2½'

16 At T-j with B1115 in Bildeston, L 'Hadleigh 5'. At the end of the village R on B1115 'Sudbury, Chelsworth, Monks Eleigh'

17 Opposite Peacock Inn in Chelsworth L 'Lindsey 2'

18 At X-roads with A1141 SA 'Lindsey 1, Boxford 6'

19 Immediately after Red Rose PH L 'By Road'

20 At T-j R (NS). At next T-j L 'Aldham 3, Hadleigh 2'

21 At X-roads with A1141 SA 'Whatfield 2, Aldham 2, Elmsett 4'

22 Steep climb. At T-j by triangle of grass R 'Aldham 1, Hadleigh 1'

◀ two pages

North from Lavenham towards Bury St Edmunds and east to the village of Rattlesden

Lavenham is the loveliest village in Suffolk and is probably best appreciated out of season. There are many fine pubs and tea shops and every street has fine old

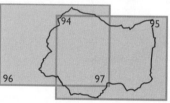

timbered buildings that are best seen on a walking tour of the village before or after the ride. The route follows the Chad Brook from Bridge Street towards Shimpling, then climbs to the dizzy heights of almost 106 m (350 ft) north of Hartest before dropping past the handsome house at Bryers near to Hawstead Green. A short section of the busy A134 is negotiated near to Sicklesmere before a steady climb towards the Nature Reserve at Bradfield Woods and the delightful church at Rattlesden. Quiet lanes take you south to the pretty thatched cottages of Kettlebaston and back to Lavenham where the climb up Prentice Street is the hardest of the day. Why not walk and take a closer look at the fine old buildings.

Start

The Tourist Information Centre, Lavenham, 16 km (10 miles) southeast of Bury St Edmunds

P Follow signs for long-stay car park just off the B1071 Sudbury road

Distance and grade

52 km (33 miles)

Easy / moderate

Terrain

Gently rolling landscape. 4 climbs of 45 m (150 ft) and several of between 15 and 30 m (50 and 100 ft). The steepest hill is right at the end as you climb Prentice Street back to the starting point. Lowest point – 42 m (140 ft) at Sicklesmere. Highest point – 100 m (330 ft) north of Hartest

Nearest railway

Bury St Edmunds, 6½ km (4 miles) northwest of the route at Sicklesmere

Lavenham

Bridge Street

Shimpling

Hartest

Hawstead

Sicklesmere

▼ *Lavenham*

Lavenham 1
Resplendent Suffolk wool town reflects the prosperous Middle Ages – the telegraph lines are hidden underground to preserve the character of over 300 listed buildings. Tudor houses sag with age and the cathedral-like church on the hill is the greatest of all East Anglia's medieval 'wool' churches. The old Wool Hall is now part of the Swan Hotel. The Museum of Weaving Industry is displayed in the Tudor Guildhall

The Priory, Lavenham 1
Medieval Benedictine Priory, later a Tudor clothier's residence. Recently rescued from a derelict ruin with a Great Hall, Jacobean staircase, courtyard, aromatic herb garden, kitchen garden, orchard and pond

Long Melford (just off the route) 3
The main street of the village runs along the former Roman highway. Pepperpot towers distinguish the 16th-century mansion of Melford Hall. The 16th-century Bull Inn is reputed to be haunted. The moated manor of Kentwell Hall has a Tudor-rose maze and rare breeds of domestic farm animals

Bradfield Woods Nature Reserve 12
A diversity of soils gives a wide variety of plants, regularly coppiced native trees and shrubs with unusual fungi in autumn. The reserve is home to four kinds of deer, small mammals, butterflies and migrant birds.

Refreshments

Plenty of choice in Lavenham
Rose and Crown PH, Bridge Street
The Crown PH ❦, Hartest
Metcalfe Arms PH, Hawstead Green
Fox and Hounds PH, Maypole Green
Brewers Arms PH, Rattlesden
Six Bells PH, Preston St Mary

Gedding

Rattlesden

Hitcham

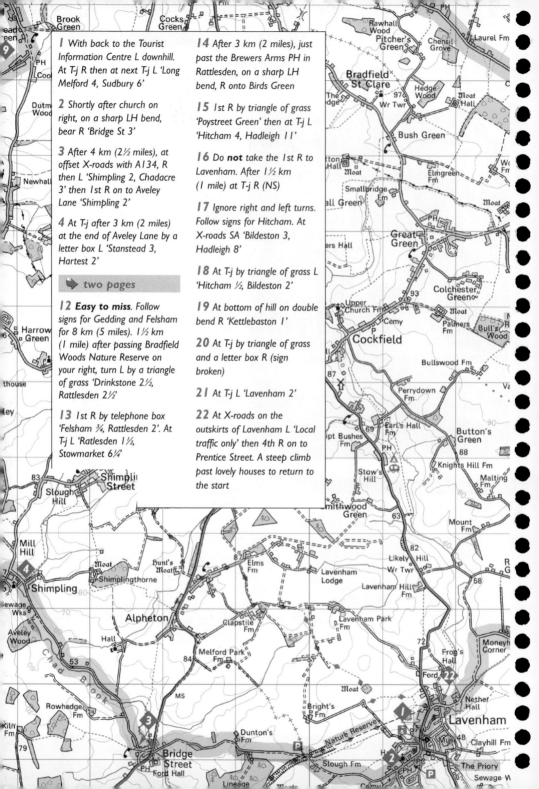

1 With back to the Tourist Information Centre L downhill. At T-j R then at next T-j L 'Long Melford 4, Sudbury 6'

2 Shortly after church on right, on a sharp LH bend, bear R 'Bridge St 3'

3 After 4 km (2½ miles), at offset X-roads with A134, R then L 'Shimpling 2, Chadacre 3' then 1st R on to Aveley Lane 'Shimpling 2'

4 At T-j after 3 km (2 miles) at the end of Aveley Lane by a letter box L 'Stanstead 3, Hartest 2'

➡ **two pages**

12 **Easy to miss.** Follow signs for Gedding and Felsham for 8 km (5 miles). 1½ km (1 mile) after passing Bradfield Woods Nature Reserve on your right, turn L by a triangle of grass 'Drinkstone 2½, Rattlesden 2½'

13 1st R by telephone box 'Felsham ¾, Rattlesden 2'. At T-j L 'Ratlesden 1½, Stowmarket 6¼'

14 After 3 km (2 miles), just past the Brewers Arms PH in Rattlesden, on a sharp LH bend, R onto Birds Green

15 1st R by triangle of grass 'Poystreet Green' then at T-j L 'Hitcham 4, Hadleigh 11'

16 Do **not** take the 1st R to Lavenham. After 1½ km (1 mile) at T-j R (NS)

17 Ignore right and left turns. Follow signs for Hitcham. At X-roads SA 'Bildeston 3, Hadleigh 8'

18 At T-j by triangle of grass L 'Hitcham ½, Bildeston 2'

19 At bottom of hill on double bend R 'Kettlebaston 1'

20 At T-j by triangle of grass and a letter box R (sign broken)

21 At T-j L 'Lavenham 2'

22 At X-roads on the outskirts of Lavenham L 'Local traffic only' then 4th R on to Prentice Street. A steep climb past lovely houses to return to the start

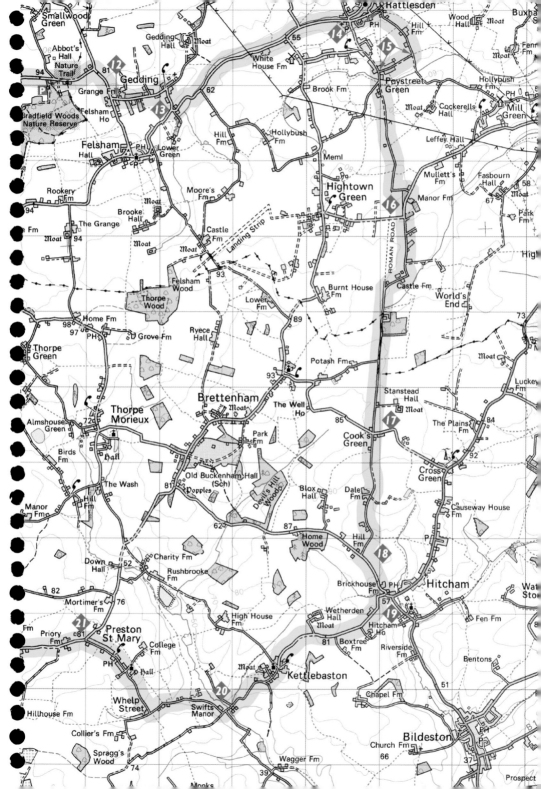

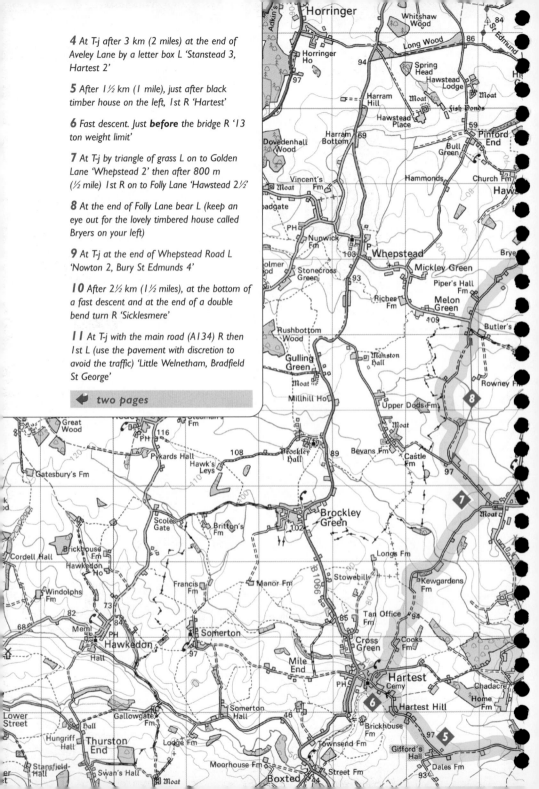

4 At T-j after 3 km (2 miles) at the end of Aveley Lane by a letter box L 'Stanstead 3, Hartest 2'

5 After 1½ km (1 mile), just after black timber house on the left, 1st R 'Hartest'

6 Fast descent. Just **before** the bridge R '13 ton weight limit'

7 At T-j by triangle of grass L on to Golden Lane 'Whepstead 2' then after 800 m (½ mile) 1st R on to Folly Lane 'Hawstead 2½'

8 At the end of Folly Lane bear L (keep an eye out for the lovely timbered house called Bryers on your left)

9 At T-j at the end of Whepstead Road L 'Nowton 2, Bury St Edmunds 4'

10 After 2½ km (1½ miles), at the bottom of a fast descent and at the end of a double bend turn R 'Sicklesmere'

11 At T-j with the main road (A134) R then 1st L (use the pavement with discretion to avoid the traffic) 'Little Welnetham, Bradfield St George'

← two pages

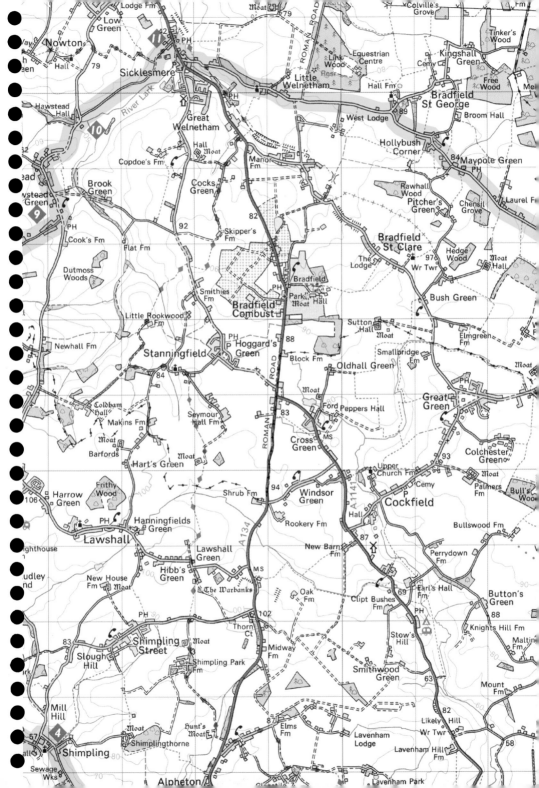

16 Through the heart of Fenland from Ely to Chatteris

Start

The Lamb Inn, near the cathedral in Ely

P Follow signs

Distance and grade

67 km (42 miles)

Easy

Terrain

Almost all near sea level: the flattest ride in a flat region!

Nearest railway

Ely

Compared to most of Great Britain, East Anglia is flat: to the east of the A1 the land rarely rises above 150m (500 ft). The northern half of East Anglia (the area covered by this book) is even flatter, rarely rising above 90m (300 ft). This ride from Ely runs across the dark soil of the fens, some of the richest and most productive agricultural land in the whole of Britain. Ely Cathedral soars above the surrounding Fenland, its scale dwarfing all around it. The limited crossings of the Wash or the Old Bedford River dictate the shape of this ride: the bridge over the river at Welney is the only road crossing for 27km (17 miles) between Mepal in the southwest and Downham Market in the northeast. The ride heads west to Coveney, passing between the rich, dark fields surrounded by drainage ditches. Remember to look behind you to see the silhouette of Ely Cathedral. The houses are almost all brick-built: there is a particularly fine old red-brick house in Witcham. Sutton offers little to detain the cyclist, but just beyond the village, the pub at Sutton Gault with its garden overlooking the river makes a fine break. Chatteris has a few old buildings in its centre, but this is above all a ride through the dark fenland and for the rest of its course it passes through nowhere bigger than the villages of Manea ('Maynee') and Little Downham, by which time you are being drawn back again to the looming shape of Ely Cathedral.

Ely · Coveney · Wardy Hill · Witcham · Sutton · North Fen · Chatteris · Horseway · Manea · Tipps End · Welney · A1101 · Pymore · Little Downham

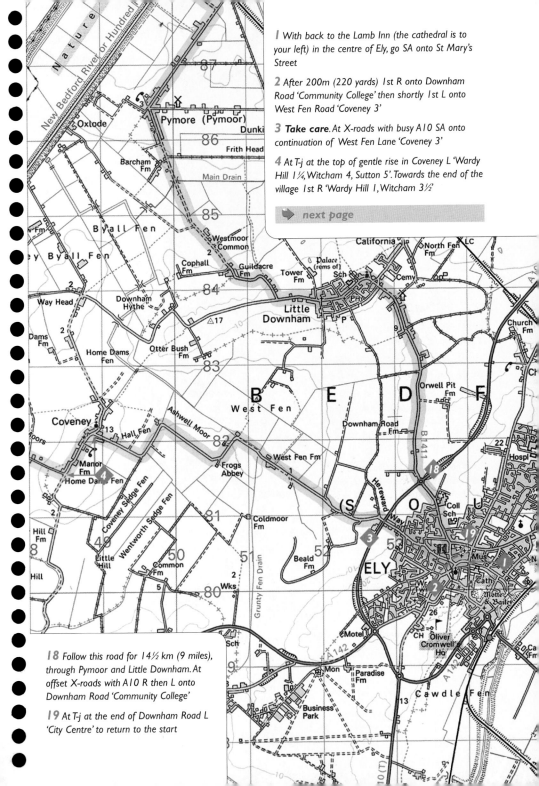

1 With back to the Lamb Inn (the cathedral is to your left) in the centre of Ely, go SA onto St Mary's Street

2 After 200m (220 yards) 1st R onto Downham Road 'Community College' then shortly 1st L onto West Fen Road 'Coveney 3'

3 *Take care.* At X-roads with busy A10 SA onto continuation of West Fen Lane 'Coveney 3'

4 At T-j at the top of gentle rise in Coveney L 'Wardy Hill 1¼, Witcham 4, Sutton 5'. Towards the end of the village 1st R 'Wardy Hill 1, Witcham 3½'

➤ *next page*

18 Follow this road for 14½ km (9 miles), through Pymoor and Little Downham. At offset X-roads with A10 R then L onto Downham Road 'Community College'

19 At T-j at the end of Downham Road L 'City Centre' to return to the start

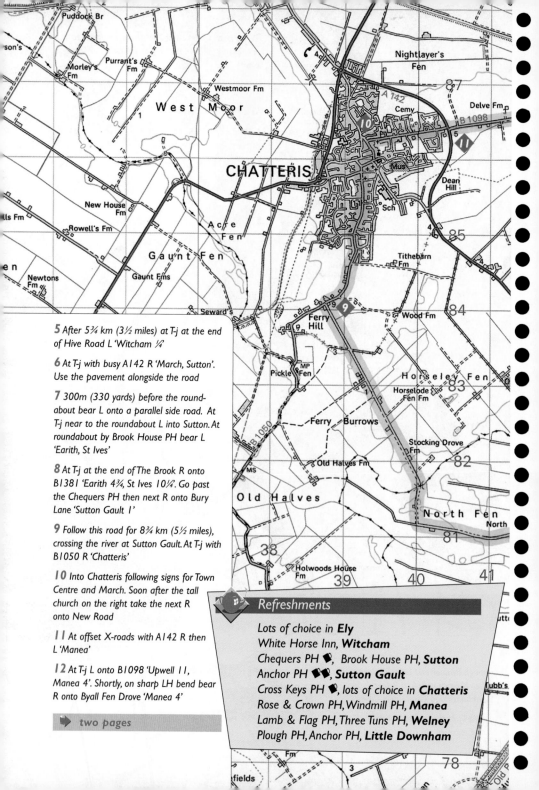

5 After 5¾ km (3½ miles) at T-j at the end of Hive Road L 'Witcham ¼'

6 At T-j with busy A142 R 'March, Sutton'. Use the pavement alongside the road

7 300m (330 yards) before the roundabout bear L onto a parallel side road. At T-j near to the roundabout L into Sutton. At roundabout by Brook House PH bear L 'Earith, St Ives'

8 At T-j at the end of The Brook R onto B1381 'Earith 4¾, St Ives 10¼'. Go past the Chequers PH then next R onto Bury Lane 'Sutton Gault 1'

9 Follow this road for 8¾ km (5½ miles), crossing the river at Sutton Gault. At T-j with B1050 R 'Chatteris'

10 Into Chatteris following signs for Town Centre and March. Soon after the tall church on the right take the next R onto New Road

11 At offset X-roads with A142 R then L 'Manea'

12 At T-j L onto B1098 'Upwell 11, Manea 4'. Shortly, on sharp LH bend bear R onto Byall Fen Drove 'Manea 4'

➡ **two pages**

Refreshments

Lots of choice in **Ely**
White Horse Inn, **Witcham**
Chequers PH 🍴, Brook House PH, **Sutton**
Anchor PH 🍴🍴, **Sutton Gault**
Cross Keys PH 🍴, lots of choice in **Chatteris**
Rose & Crown PH, Windmill PH, **Manea**
Lamb & Flag PH, Three Tuns PH, **Welney**
Plough PH, Anchor PH, **Little Downham**

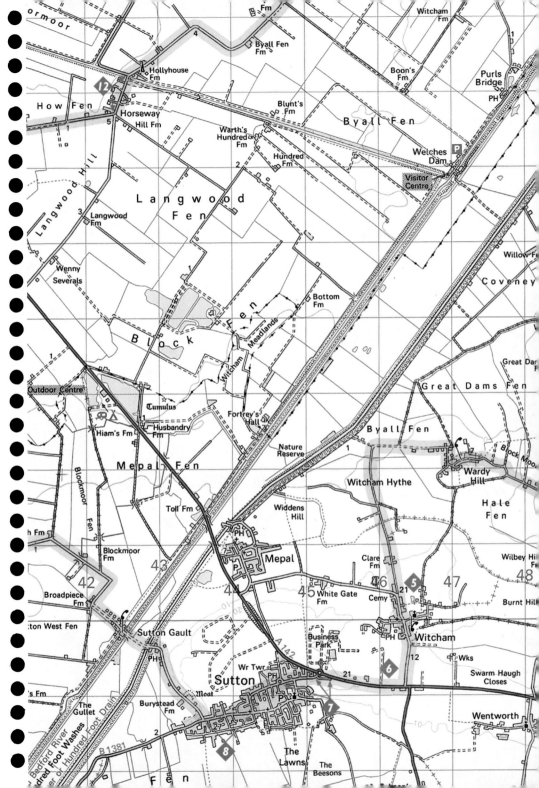

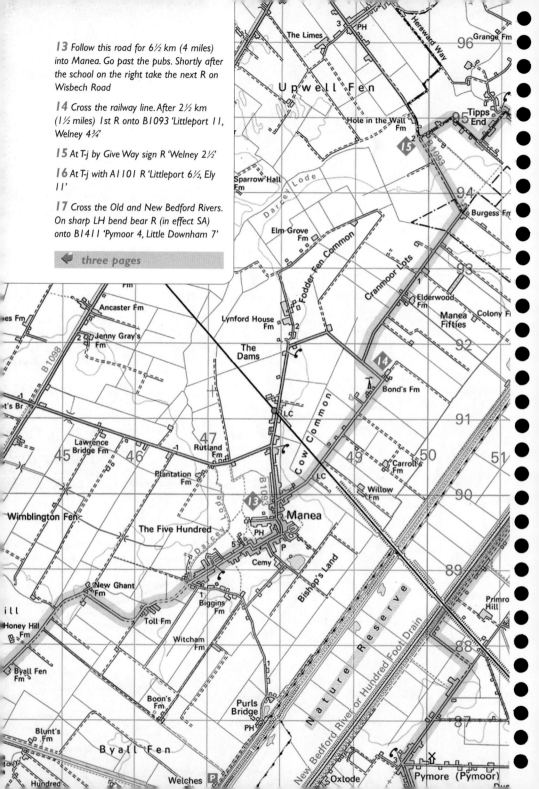

13 Follow this road for 6½ km (4 miles) into Manea. Go past the pubs. Shortly after the school on the right take the next R on Wisbech Road

14 Cross the railway line. After 2½ km (1½ miles) 1st R onto B1093 'Littleport 11, Welney 4¾'

15 At T-j by Give Way sign R 'Welney 2½'

16 At T-j with A1101 R 'Littleport 6½, Ely 11'

17 Cross the Old and New Bedford Rivers. On sharp LH bend bear R (in effect SA) onto B1411 'Pymoor 4, Little Downham 7'

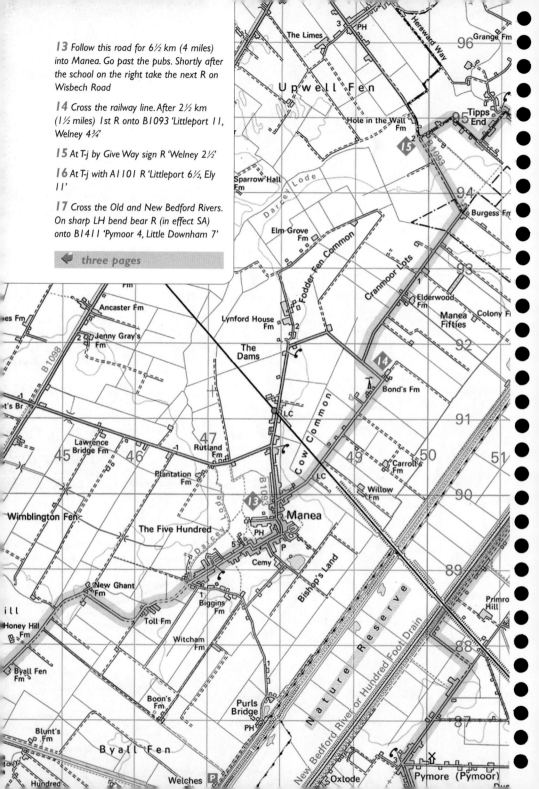 three pages

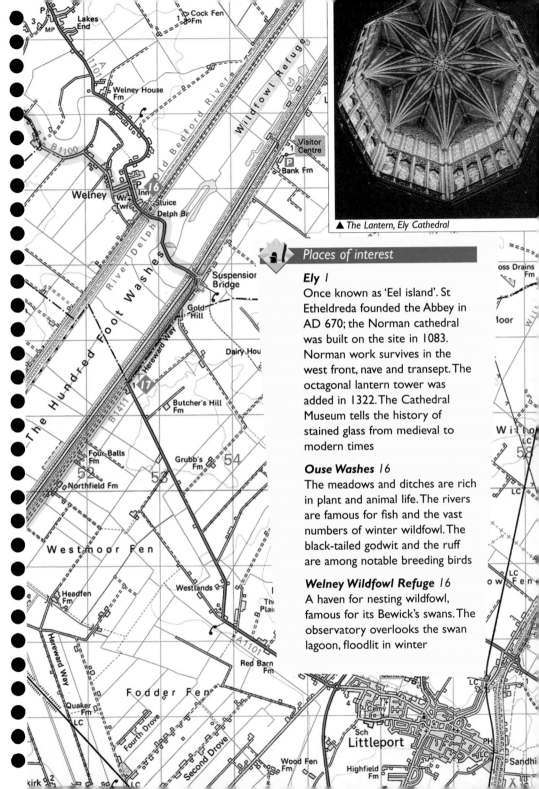

▲ *The Lantern, Ely Cathedral*

Places of interest

Ely 1
Once known as 'Eel island'. St Etheldreda founded the Abbey in AD 670; the Norman cathedral was built on the site in 1083. Norman work survives in the west front, nave and transept. The octagonal lantern tower was added in 1322. The Cathedral Museum tells the history of stained glass from medieval to modern times

Ouse Washes 16
The meadows and ditches are rich in plant and animal life. The rivers are famous for fish and the vast numbers of winter wildfowl. The black-tailed godwit and the ruff are among notable breeding birds

Welney Wildfowl Refuge 16
A haven for nesting wildfowl, famous for its Bewick's swans. The observatory overlooks the swan lagoon, floodlit in winter

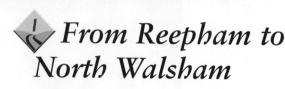 # From Reepham to North Walsham along the Marriotts Way and Weavers Way

So often the disused railways have been sold off piecemeal to adjacent landowners. By luck, this one was running until as recently as 1985 and so has not suffered in the same way. The attractive town of Aylsham is the link between the two separate paths: it is explored on the outward leg, the return trip using an off-road link skirting the north of the town. The quality of the surface varies: on the Marriotts Way, between Reepham and Aylsham, a narrow section has been improved with compacted aggregate, although it is rarely wide enough to ride two abreast. Beyond Aylsham the surface is slightly rougher but not segregated into horse and bike sections. There is a wide variety of wildflowers along both paths.

 Start

The old railway station at Reepham, 20 km (12 miles) northwest of Norwich

P As above. The entrance to the Old Railway Station is 1¼ km (¾ mile) north of the crossroads in the centre of Reepham on the B1145 towards Aylsham (opposite the Crown PH)

 Distance and grade

21 km (13 miles) one way

  Moderate

Terrain

Dismantled railway path with mixture of embankments and cuttings with rich variety of wildflowers. No hills. The surface varies but should be passable to hybrid and mountain bikes

 Reepham

 Cawston

Nearest railway

North Walsham

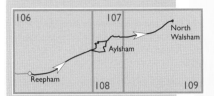

106   107   North Walsham
       Aylsham
Reepham
108   109

Places of interest

Reepham 1

An 18th-century market town with Georgian houses and half-timbered dwellings, where three churches used to share a single churchyard. Two remain — they are linked by the choir vestry. One has been a ruin since 1543. There is a sundial over the door of the Georgian Old Brewery

Aylsham 2–3

A market town with splendid old buildings: the Manor House and Abbots Hall date from the early 1600s and the Old Hall from 1689. The rose-covered grave of the landscape gardener Humphry Repton lies in the churchyard of the 14th-century St Michael's Church

Blickling Hall 1 mile north of 13

A Jacobean 17th-century moated hall with an immaculate formal garden and impressive imperial period-style rooms.

Refreshments:

Kings Arms PH 🍺, Old Brewery House PH 🍺, lots of choice in **Reepham**
Refreshments just off the route in **Cawston**
Greens PH 🍺, lots of choice in **Aylsham**
Bluebell PH 🍺, lots of choice in
North Walsham

▼ Blickling Hall

1 From the Reepham Station car park descend to the railway line and turn R (east)

2 At T-j (with B1354) opposite the Bure Valley Railway Station in Aylsham turn L. Follow road round to the L then take next R through Market Square towards Town Hall

3 At T-j L 'Ingworth' then 1st R onto White Hart Street 'Tuttington. Bypass'

4 Past the Stonemasons Arms PH. Cross the river then 1st L onto one way street. Cross railway bridge, 1st R onto Banningham Road, then 1st L onto continuation of Banningham Road 'Weavers Way'

5 **Ignore** 1st right (no through road). Take next R onto track at X-roads with 'No through road' sign ahead. At X-roads with busy A140 SA onto track. This section may be rough

6 At T-j with a better, stone-based track R then L to join the dismantled railway line. Follow for 6½ km (4 miles)

➡ next page

10 At the end of the dismantled railway track, with a house ahead, R then 1st track L 'No through road'. Rough section

11 At T-j with the busy A140 SA onto track. At cross-roads with tarmac L

12 At T-j at the end of Banningham Road sharp R (ie not the main road). After 50 yards L into gravel car park then R onto railway path. Follow for 1¼ km (¾ mile)

13 At T-j (with the B1354) SA. Short, steep climb. At T-j with tarmac path L and follow this parallel to the road

14 **Easy to miss.** Opposite handsome red-brick house turn R 'Weavers Way' through gap in fence just beyond stile then R through bridlegate. Follow grassy track through the long narrow field opposite the house

15 Just before the end of the field bear L through bridlegate. At T-j with the road L then 1st track R by a red-brick house

16 At start of tarmac, as lane swings L, bear R (in effect SA) 'Marriotts Way / Weavers Way Link'. At T-j with road L then immediately R onto Marriotts Way to rejoin outward route for 8 km (5 miles) back to Reepham

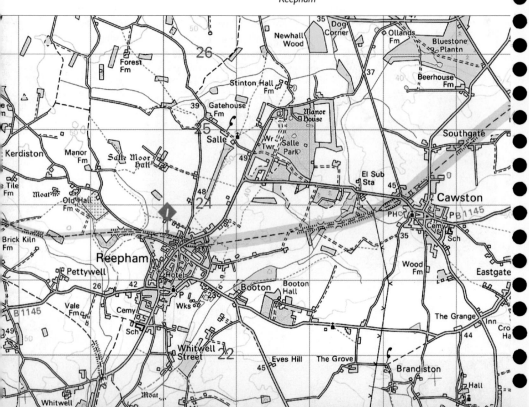

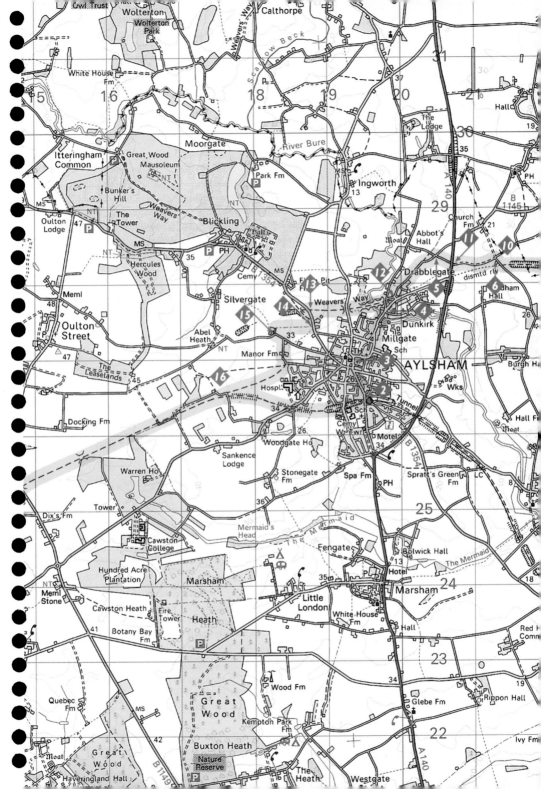

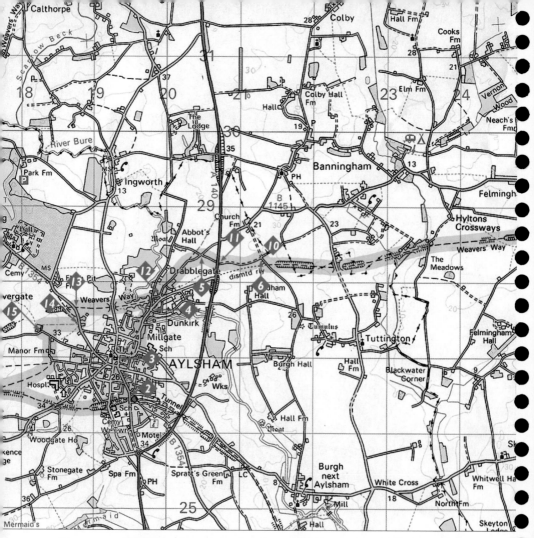

2 At T-j (with B1354) opposite the Bure Valley Railway Station in Aylsham turn L. Follow road round to the L then take next R through Market Square towards Town Hall

3 At T-j L 'Ingworth' then 1st R onto White Hart Street 'Tuttington. Bypass'

4 Past the Stonemasons Arms PH. Cross the river then 1st L onto one way street. Cross railway bridge, 1st R onto Banningham Road, then 1st L onto continuation of Banningham Road 'Weavers Way'

5 Ignore 1st right (no through road). Take next R onto track at X-roads with 'No through road' sign ahead. At X-roads with busy A140 SA onto track. This section may be rough

6 At T-j with a better, stone-based track R then L to join the dismantled railway line. Follow for 6½ km (4 miles)

7 On the outskirts of North Walsham, at X-roads with Station Road at the end of the railway path SA onto lane opposite. At T-j R under railway bridge and follow the one way system around to the R to the Market Cross in the centre of North Walsham

8 From the Market Cross in North Walsham take Kings Arms Street past the Kings Arms Hotel sign-posted 'A149, B1150'. At the end of the road turn R then stay in the LH lane, following signs for Aylsham

▲ Weavers' Way near North Walsham

9 Immediately after passing beneath the road and railway bridges turn L (NS). At T-j (with Station Road) SA onto track 'Weavers Way'. Follow for 6½ km (4 miles)

10 At the end of the dismantled railway track, with a house ahead, R then 1st track L 'No through road'. Rough section

11 At T-j with the busy A140 SA onto track. At crossroads with tarmac L

12 At T-j at the end of Banningham Road sharp R (ie not the main road). After 45m (50 yards) L into gravel car park then R onto railway path. Follow for 1¼ km (¾ mile)

13 At T-j (with the B1354) SA. Short, steep climb. At T-j with tarmac path L and follow this parallel to the road

14 **Easy to miss.** Opposite handsome red-brick house turn R 'Weavers Way' through gap in fence just beyond stile then R through bridlegate. Follow grassy track through the long narrow field opposite the house

15 Just before the end of the field bear L through bridlegate. At T-j with the road L then 1st track R by a red-brick house

 three pages

The Marriotts Way from Norwich to Reepham

Start

The Tourist Information Centre, the Guildhall, Market Square, Norwich

P There are car parks on Oak Street, off St Crispins, in the centre of Norwich. However, if arriving by car it might be better to consider starting in Drayton.

With little time spent on the traffic-filled streets of Norwich, and with cycle lanes and well-placed pelican crossings to help you negotiate the busy roads, it is possible to escape quickly and safely from the middle of the city to the heart of the countryside on a series of excellently maintained and well-signposted connecting trails. It is surprising how close one passes to built-up areas and industrial estates while still maintaining the impression of being in a rural setting. The woodlands of Mileplain Plantation are a real delight: a deep cutting planted with sweet chestnut trees, especially attractive during the changing autumn colours. The whole route is studded with a wide variety of broadleaf trees – oak, ash, hawthorn, silver birch and sycamore. The clear, gently-flowing waters of the River Wensum are crossed three times on fine old metal bridges with wooden planking. Between Lenwade and Reepham you have the option of the full route following the Themelthorpe Loop or taking a shortcut which saves 6½ km (4 miles). The loop and shortcut could be made into a separate 11 km (7 mile) ride from Reepham.

Refreshments

*Lots of choice in **Norwich** Kings Arms PH 🍺, Old Brewery House PH 🍺, lots of choice in **Reepham** Refreshments off the route in **Drayton** and **Lenwade***

Norwich

A1067

Freeland Corner

Distance and grade

30 km (19 miles) one
way Norwich–Lenwade
–Themelthorpe–Reep-
ham or 22 km
(14 miles) using short-
cut near Reepham

Moderate

Terrain

Easy, flat railway trail
from the heart of the
city through wooded
cuttings and along
embankments above
arable land. Lowest
point – 5m (16 ft) at
the River Wensum in
Norwich. Highest point
– 50m (165 ft) at
Themelthorpe

Nearest railway

Norwich

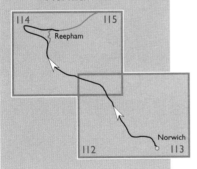

Places of interest

Norwich 1

East Anglia's flourishing capital has one of
the country's most beautiful cathedrals,
and the city centre which boasts some
30 medieval churches is dominated by
Norwich Castle. Museums abound: there
are archaeology and art galleries in the
castle; the medieval Stranger's Hall has
period rooms depicting domestic life
from Tudor to Victorian times

▲ *The Marriotts Way near Reepham*

Lenwade   Blackwater   Themelthorpe   Reepham

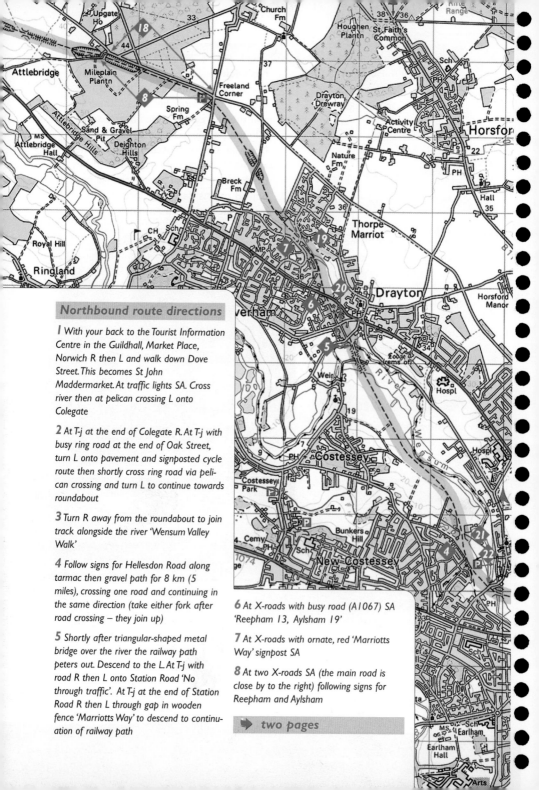

Northbound route directions

1 With your back to the Tourist Information Centre in the Guildhall, Market Place, Norwich R then L and walk down Dove Street. This becomes St John Maddermarket. At traffic lights SA. Cross river then at pelican crossing L onto Colegate

2 At T-j at the end of Colegate R. At T-j with busy ring road at the end of Oak Street, turn L onto pavement and signposted cycle route then shortly cross ring road via pelican crossing and turn L to continue towards roundabout

3 Turn R away from the roundabout to join track alongside the river 'Wensum Valley Walk'

4 Follow signs for Hellesdon Road along tarmac then gravel path for 8 km (5 miles), crossing one road and continuing in the same direction (take either fork after road crossing – they join up)

5 Shortly after triangular-shaped metal bridge over the river the railway path peters out. Descend to the L. At T-j with road R then L onto Station Road 'No through traffic'. At T-j at the end of Station Road R then L through gap in wooden fence 'Marriotts Way' to descend to continuation of railway path

6 At X-roads with busy road (A1067) SA 'Reepham 13, Aylsham 19'

7 At X-roads with ornate, red 'Marriotts Way' signpost SA

8 At two X-roads SA (the main road is close by to the right) following signs for Reepham and Aylsham

➡ two pages

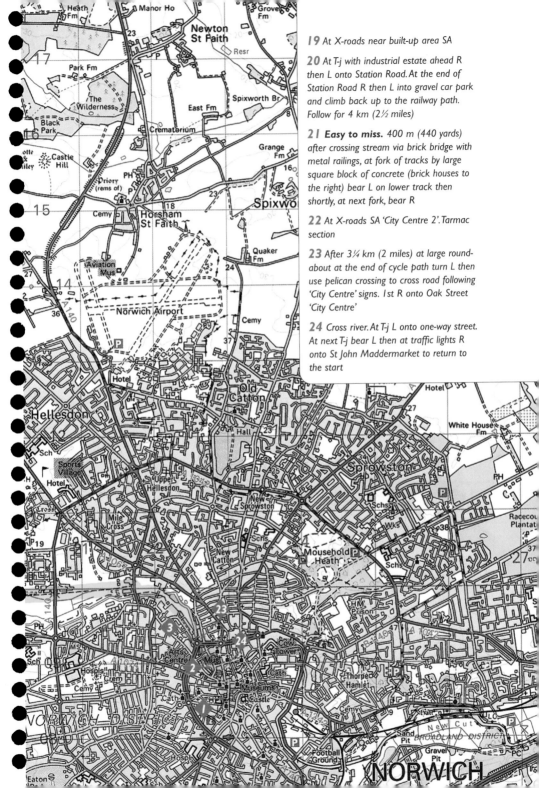

19 At X-roads near built-up area SA

20 At T-j with industrial estate ahead R then L onto Station Road. At the end of Station Road R then L into gravel car park and climb back up to the railway path. Follow for 4 km (2½ miles)

21 *Easy to miss.* 400 m (440 yards) after crossing stream via brick bridge with metal railings, at fork of tracks by large square block of concrete (brick houses to the right) bear L on lower track then shortly, at next fork, bear R

22 At X-roads SA 'City Centre 2'. Tarmac section

23 After 3¼ km (2 miles) at large round-about at the end of cycle path turn L then use pelican crossing to cross road following 'City Centre' signs. 1st R onto Oak Street 'City Centre'

24 Cross river. At T-j L onto one-way street. At next T-j bear L then at traffic lights R onto St John Maddermarket to return to the start

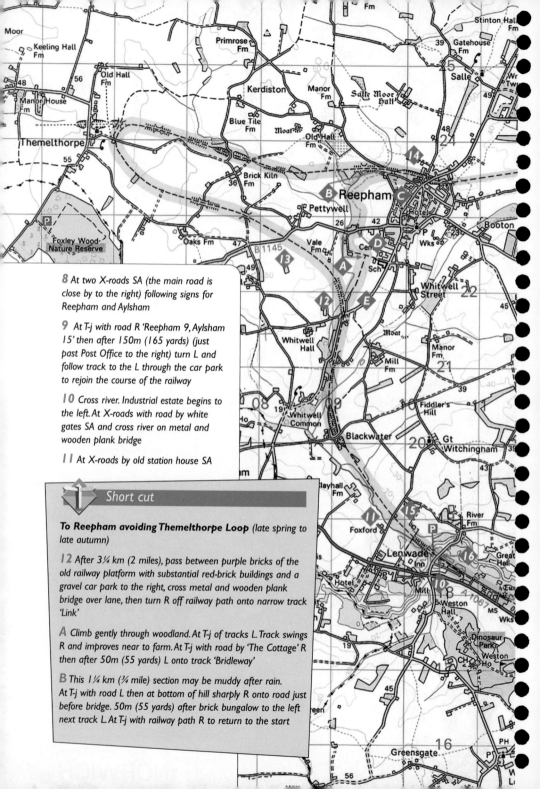

8 At two X-roads SA (the main road is close by to the right) following signs for Reepham and Aylsham

9 At T-j with road R 'Reepham 9, Aylsham 15' then after 150m (165 yards) (just past Post Office to the right) turn L and follow track to the L through the car park to rejoin the course of the railway

10 Cross river. Industrial estate begins to the left. At X-roads with road by white gates SA and cross river on metal and wooden plank bridge

11 At X-roads by old station house SA

Short cut

To Reepham avoiding Themelthorpe Loop (late spring to late autumn)

12 After 3¼ km (2 miles), pass between purple bricks of the old railway platform with substantial red-brick buildings and a gravel car park to the right, cross metal and wooden plank bridge over lane, then turn R off railway path onto narrow track 'Link'

A Climb gently through woodland. At T-j of tracks L. Track swings R and improves near to farm. At T-j with road by 'The Cottage' R then after 50m (55 yards) L onto track 'Bridleway'

B This 1¼ km (¾ mile) section may be muddy after rain. At T-j with road L then at bottom of hill sharply R onto road just before bridge. 50m (55 yards) after brick bungalow to the left next track L. At T-j with railway path R to return to the start

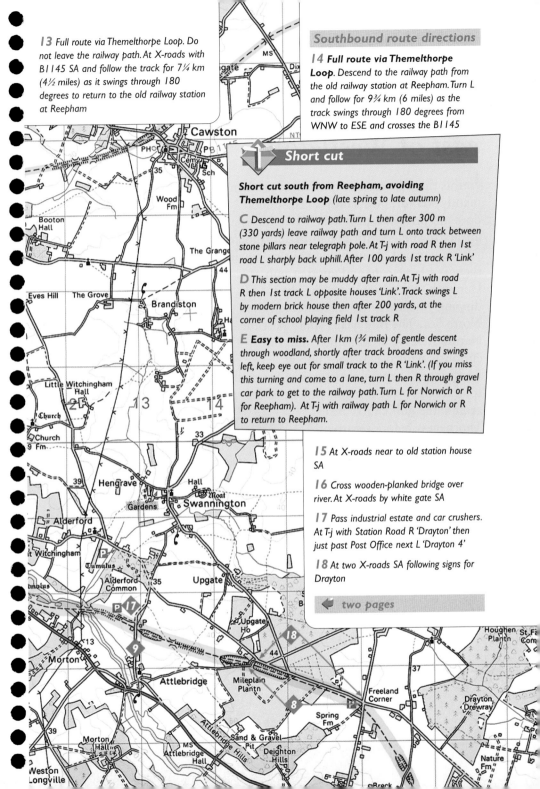

13 Full route via Themelthorpe Loop. Do not leave the railway path. At X-roads with B1145 SA and follow the track for 7¼ km (4½ miles) as it swings through 180 degrees to return to the old railway station at Reepham

14 Full route via Themelthorpe Loop. Descend to the railway path from the old railway station at Reepham. Turn L and follow for 9¾ km (6 miles) as the track swings through 180 degrees from WNW to ESE and crosses the B1145

Short cut

Short cut south from Reepham, avoiding Themelthorpe Loop (late spring to late autumn)

C Descend to railway path. Turn L then after 300 m (330 yards) leave railway path and turn L onto track between stone pillars near telegraph pole. At T-j with road R then 1st road L sharply back uphill. After 100 yards 1st track R 'Link'

D This section may be muddy after rain. At T-j with road R then 1st track L opposite houses 'Link'. Track swings L by modern brick house then after 200 yards, at the corner of school playing field 1st track R

E Easy to miss. After 1km (¾ mile) of gentle descent through woodland, shortly after track broadens and swings left, keep eye out for small track to the R 'Link'. (If you miss this turning and come to a lane, turn L then R through gravel car park to get to the railway path. Turn L for Norwich or R for Reepham). At T-j with railway path L for Norwich or R to return to Reepham.

15 At X-roads near to old station house SA

16 Cross wooden-planked bridge over river. At X-roads by white gate SA

17 Pass industrial estate and car crushers. At T-j with Station Road R 'Drayton' then just past Post Office next L 'Drayton 4'

18 At two X-roads SA following signs for Drayton

two pages

3 A figure of eight loop on the Suffolk Coast heathland east of Westleton

In this ride, the terrain consists of predominantly well-drained sandy soils, so mud does not present a problem. Westleton is an attractive village with fine pubs and should you be worried about filling your stomach, there is a large café and another pub at Dunwich, where you have the chance of dipping your toes into the waters of the North Sea. The ride heads south past the Nature Reserve at Minsmere and the curiously named Eels Foot pub at Eastbridge. The vast structures of Sizewell soon loom on the horizon. A loop is drawn around the golf course near Thorpeness before returning north back to Westleton.

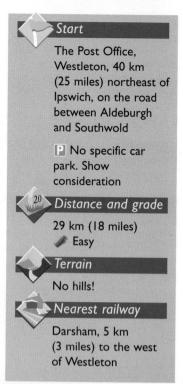

Start

The Post Office, Westleton, 40 km (25 miles) northeast of Ipswich, on the road between Aldeburgh and Southwold

P No specific car park. Show consideration

Distance and grade

29 km (18 miles)

Easy

Terrain

No hills!

Nearest railway

Darsham, 5 km (3 miles) to the west of Westleton

Refreshments

The Crown PH ♥♥, The White Horse PH ♥, **Westleton** Ship Inn PH, Café on the beach, **Dunwich**
Eels Foot PH ♥, **Eastbridge**
Vulcan Arms PH, **Sizewell**

Westleton   Dunwich   Eastbridge   Leiston Common

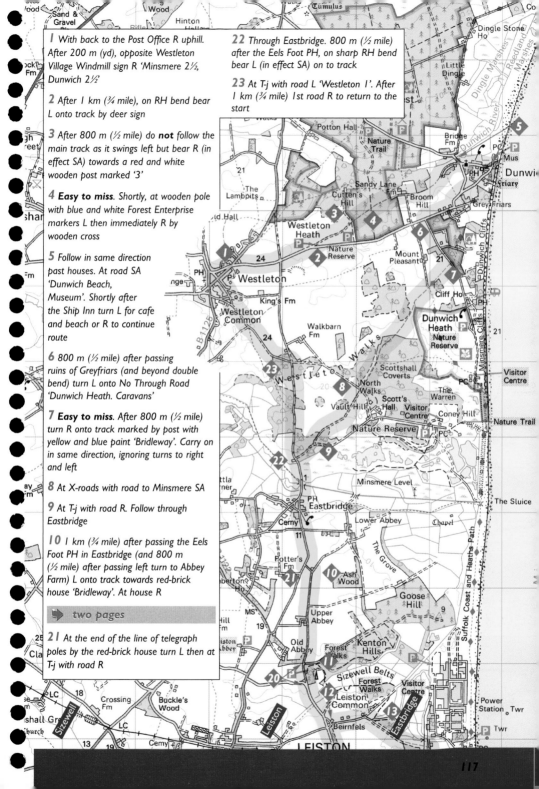

1 With back to the Post Office R uphill. After 200 m (yd), opposite Westleton Village Windmill sign R 'Minsmere 2½, Dunwich 2½'

2 After 1 km (¾ mile), on RH bend bear L onto track by deer sign

3 After 800 m (½ mile) do **not** follow the main track as it swings left but bear R (in effect SA) towards a red and white wooden post marked '3'

4 **Easy to miss**. Shortly, at wooden pole with blue and white Forest Enterprise markers L then immediately R by wooden cross

5 Follow in same direction past houses. At road SA 'Dunwich Beach, Museum'. Shortly after the Ship Inn turn L for cafe and beach or R to continue route

6 800 m (½ mile) after passing ruins of Greyfriars (and beyond double bend) turn L onto No Through Road 'Dunwich Heath. Caravans'

7 **Easy to miss**. After 800 m (½ mile) turn R onto track marked by post with yellow and blue paint 'Bridleway'. Carry on in same direction, ignoring turns to right and left

8 At X-roads with road to Minsmere SA

9 At T-j with road R. Follow through Eastbridge

10 1 km (¾ mile) after passing the Eels Foot PH in Eastbridge (and 800 m (½ mile) after passing left turn to Abbey Farm) L onto track towards red-brick house 'Bridleway'. At house R

➡ **two pages**

21 At the end of the line of telegraph poles by the red-brick house turn L then at T-j with road R

22 Through Eastbridge. 800 m (½ mile) after the Eels Foot PH, on sharp RH bend bear L (in effect SA) on to track

23 At T-j with road L 'Westleton 1'. After 1 km (¾ mile) 1st road R to return to the start

10 I km (¾ mile) after passing the Eels Foot PH in Eastbridge (and 800 m (½ mile) after passing left turn to Abbey Farm) L onto track towards
red-brick house 'Bridleway'. At house R

11 At T-j with more major track bear R then at T-j with road L

12 At top of short hill, just before X-roads sign, bear L then after 50 m (yd) turn L onto broad gravel track 'Bridleway'

13 After 400 m (¼ mile) leave broad gravel track by triangle of grass and bear R onto sandy track 'Bridleway'

14 At T-j immediately after going beneath power lines R. At T-j with road L then R 'Sizewell Hall'

15 Tarmac turns to track. After 800 m (½ mile) fork R 'Byway'. Continue on main track in same direction. At T-j with road R

16 After 800 (½ mile), just after the telephone lines cross from the road from one side to the other R onto broad track. Take the middle of the three tracks

17 Follow the broad track as it swings right by the remarkable red-brick Providence Baptist Church then L alongside golf course

18 At the end of a row of houses bear L onto narrow grassy track. Go beneath power lines At T-j with major track R and follow this past Crownlands Cottage as it swings left to the road

19 At road junction bear L 'Yoxford, Saxmundham (A12)'

20 After 1½ km (1 mile), at top of short hill on LH bend by mast, turn R onto broad gravel track. Shortly after car park bear L (in effect SA) off the main track

21 At the end of the line of telegraph poles by the red-brick house turn L then at T-j with road R

 two pages

▲ The beach at Dunwich

Places of interest

Westleton Heath 2
Sandy heaths, woodland, heather and bracken with bird life including stone curlews, nightjars, red-backed shrikes and woodlarks

Dunwich 5
The relentless erosion of wind and tide caused this town to be lost beneath the waves after a huge storm in 1326. Only a small village, the ruins of a leper chapel and a medieval friary remain of what was once the capital of the Saxon Kingdom of East Anglia. It is said that submerged bells ring out a storm warning. There is an excellent museum on the town's history

Minsmere 9
A major bird reserve with nesting places for over 100 species. Breeding birds include avocets, bitterns, nightjars and nightingales

Thorpeness (just off the route) 15
Eccentric holiday village, planned before World War I, surrounding a specially created 65-acre lake called the Meare. One of the town's most distinctive buildings is the extraordinary House in the Clouds. It looks like a mock-Tudor building but beneath the facade is a water tower on stilts

Byways and Roman Roads east from Fulbourn near Cambridge

*T*he best is left till last in this ride with a 11 km (7 mile) section on the Roman Road of Worstead Street, which constitutes one of the finest stretches of off-road cycling in the whole of East Anglia: the track rises and falls on gently undulating country through a canopy of trees and among a carpet of wildflowers. The surface is excellent and it seems that the local authority has taken a real pride in maintaining this length to an exceptionally high standard. The ride starts from the bustling village of Fulbourn and heads northeast, then east along quiet lanes and byways to cross the A11 and the railway line. There is a remarkable sense of remoteness about parts of this ride, given its proximity to Cambridge. Turning south, the ride follows further byways through Balsham. At the second crossing of the B1052 you are faced with a decision – tea at the Chilford Hall Vineyard or straight ahead onto the Roman Road back to Fulbourn? With luck you should have time for both

Start

The Church, Fulbourn, 6½ km (4 miles) east of Cambridge

P Large car park at Fulbourn recreation ground behind the scout hut. From the Post Office go SA onto Manor Walk towards Balsham. Go past the Townley Memorial Hall and take the next L 'Fulbourn Institute'

Distance and grade

37 km (23 miles)
Easy

Terrain

82 m (270 ft) climb from the start to Hungry Hill. Lowest point – 9 m (30 ft) just north of Fulbourn. Highest point 110 m (365 ft) just south of Balsham

Nearest railway

Dullingham 3 km (2 miles) north of the route at Underwood Hall

Fulbourn

Cambridge Hill

Places of interest

Fulbourn 1
Reed-thatched houses line the streets of the village. The 13th-century church is only one of two in England dedicated to St Vigor. To the east of the village is Fleam Dyke, a massive 7th-century earthwork built to defend East Anglia against the Mercians

Great Wilbraham 2
In the 7th century, King Penda successfully marched against East Anglia and named this area after his daughter 'Wilburgh'

Swaffham Bulbeck (north of the route at Great Wilbraham) 2
A Dutch-style Merchant's House, granary and malt house remain from its 17th-century past as an inland port. The Italian portable altar in the 13th-century church is 500 years old. The pew-ends have 15th-century carvings of fabulous beasts

Refreshments

Six Bells PH, White Hart PH, **Fulbourn** *Carpenters Arms PH,* **Great Wilbraham** *Black Bull PH, The Bell PH,* **Balsham** *Teashop at* **Chilford Hall Vineyard** *(just off the route between Balsham and Linton)*

Chilford Hall Vineyard 15
18-acre vineyard with tours, wine tastings and a tea shop

Worsted Street (Roman Road) 17
A Roman link between the trading town of Cambridge and the major Roman Road from London (now the A11)

Wandlebury *(just off the route southwest of Fulbourn)* 18
The Gog Magog hills are crowned by an Iron Age fort whose ramparts enclose 15 acres. The hills take their name from a Romano-British giant who appears in legend, sometimes as one person, Gogmagog, sometimes as two, Gog and Magog. The nearby building is a stable block of the now-demolished mansion. The famous Arab stallion Elpappo was buried beneath the central arch in 1753

Balsham

Worsted Lodge

1 With back to the church R towards the Wilbrahams and Bottisham

2 Shortly after passing the Carpenters Arms PH in Great Wilbraham, on sharp LH bend R onto High Street then shortly R again onto Butt Lane

3 Pass around a metal gate 'No cars' then shortly fork L

4 At X-roads with road SA

5 At T-j with better track by telegraph poles R to cross A11 via bridge

6 At X-roads with road (A1304) SA 'Uneven crossing. Risk of grounding'

7 At X-roads R 'Six Mile Bottom 3, Weston Colville 3'

8 At X-roads SA 'Balsham 4, Linton 7'

9 After 1 km (¾ mile), on sharp LH bend shortly after double bend sign R onto track 'Byway. Icknield Way'. On bend by large blue storage tank bear L following telegraph poles

10 At X-roads with road SA 'Byway'

11 At X-roads with road by house and barn SA

12 Track becomes tarmac. At T-j with B1052 by triangle of grass with two trees turn L (**or** to avoid rough section, turn R on B1052 for 1½ km (1 mile) then R onto 'Roman Road Walk' and rejoin at instruction 15)

13 After 400 m (¼ mile), shortly after sharp RH bend by the Post Office (and before the Black Bull PH) R onto Woodhall Lane 'No Through Road' 'Icknield Way' (sections may be rough)

14 At T-j of tracks at the bottom of hill by telegraph poles turn R (sections may be rough)

15 At X-roads with road SA 'Byway' 'Roman Road Walk' (**or** L for tea at Chilford Hall Vineyard)

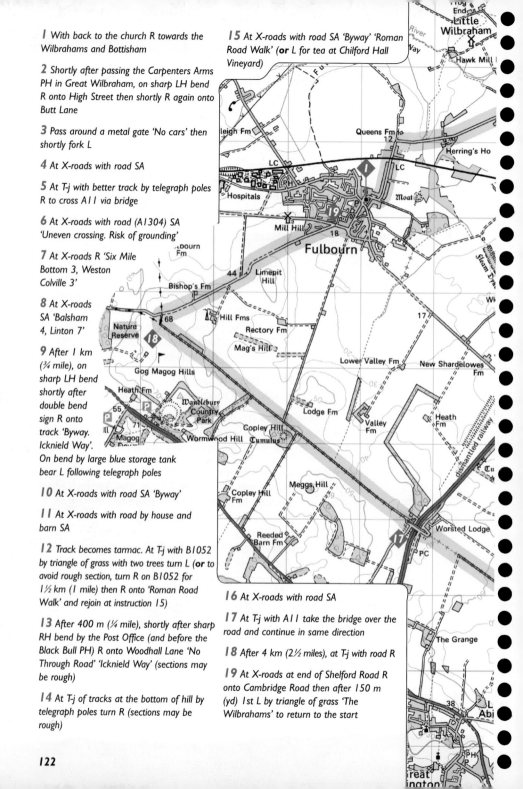

16 At X-roads with road SA

17 At T-j with A11 take the bridge over the road and continue in same direction

18 After 4 km (2½ miles), at T-j with road R

19 At X-roads at end of Shelford Road R onto Cambridge Road then after 150 m (yd) 1st L by triangle of grass 'The Wilbrahams' to return to the start

5 *Two waymarked forest routes on the Forestry Commission land near Thetford*

Draw a line 16 km (9 miles) around Thetford and you have some of the most consistently rideable offroad tracks in all of East Anglia: the soil has a sandy base and drains well and as the land is not good enough for farming, most of it is owned by the Forestry Commission and planted with pine trees. The forestry tracks around the plantations tend to have excellent all-year round surfaces and it is possible to devise any number of loops using these tracks. However, as is the case with all forestry land, it is almost impossible to give detailed route instructions when the only landmarks are trees and more trees, so the rides described are those that the Forestry Commision has already waymarked.

Start
High Lodge, on the Forest Drive south of the B1107 between Brandon and Thetford. OS National Grid reference TL811852

🅿 As above

Distance and grade
20km (13 miles) in two loops, each of 10 km (6½ miles)

🖊 Easy

Terrain
Well-waymarked tracks along sand and gravel tracks through conifer plantations. No hills.

Nearest railway
Brandon, 5 km (3 miles) north of the route at 5

Route instructions are given as a back-up to avoid getting lost. Even so, it is no bad idea to carry a compass with you so that you know in which direction you are travelling. Getting lost in Thetford Forest is hardly a life-threatening experience: you are never more than 3 km (2 miles) from a road, so if you do lose your way either retrace your steps to where you last knew where you were or continue in a straight line until you find a road and you should soon be able to re-orientate yourself.

Downham Highlodge Warren

High Wrong Corner

Mayday Farm

Places of interest

Brandon *5 km (3 miles) west of the start*
A town much admired for its buildings made of flint from local mines. There is an excellent example of flint and red brickwork on the 18th-century Brandon Hall

Refreshments

*Teas and coffees at the **Visitor Centre**
Lots of choice in **Brandon** and
Thetford*

Thetford *5 km (3 miles) southeast of the start*
The East Anglian capital of the Danes in the 9th century. There are extensive ruins of the 12th-century priory. Castle Hill has Iron Age earthworks and a Norman castle mound. The church is part Saxon, part Norman. There are medieval and Georgian buildings in almost every street. The 15th-century Ancient House houses the local and natural history museum

Grime's Graves *4½ km (3 miles) north of the start*
Visitors can descend about 10m (30 ft), by ladder, into an excavated shaft of these Neolithic flint mines and look along the radiating galleries from which the flint for making knives and axes was extracted. The site is unique in England and comprises more than 300 pits and shafts

▼ *Thetford Priory*

Brandon Country Park Visitor Centre

Mayday Farm

Session Heath

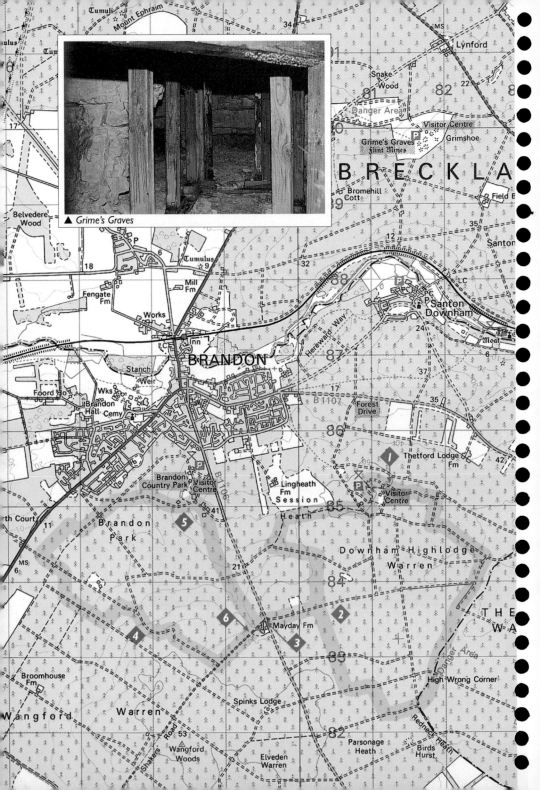

▲ Grime's Graves

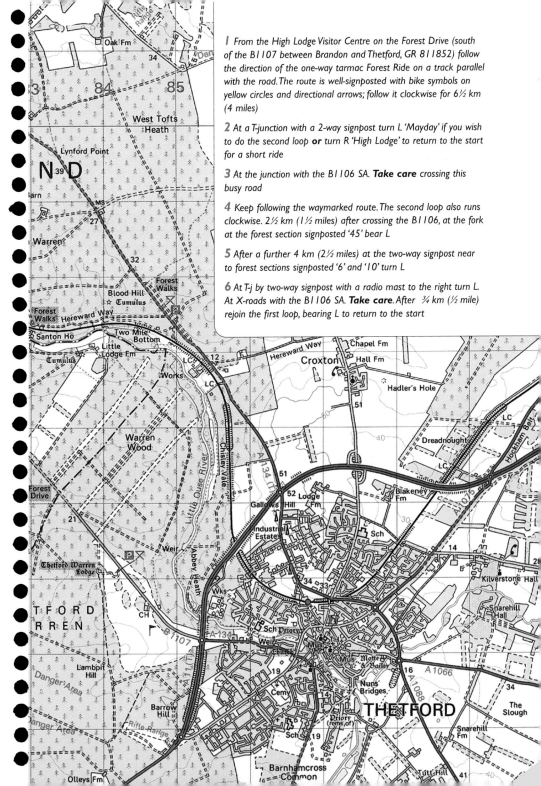

1 From the High Lodge Visitor Centre on the Forest Drive (south of the B1107 between Brandon and Thetford, GR 811852) follow the direction of the one-way tarmac Forest Ride on a track parallel with the road. The route is well-signposted with bike symbols on yellow circles and directional arrows; follow it clockwise for 6½ km (4 miles)

2 At a T-junction with a 2-way signpost turn L 'Mayday' if you wish to do the second loop **or** turn R 'High Lodge' to return to the start for a short ride

3 At the junction with the B1106 SA. **Take care** crossing this busy road

4 Keep following the waymarked route. The second loop also runs clockwise. 2½ km (1½ miles) after crossing the B1106, at the fork at the forest section signposted '45' bear L

5 After a further 4 km (2½ miles) at the two-way signpost near to forest sections signposted '6' and '10' turn L

6 At T-j by two-way signpost with a radio mast to the right turn L. At X-roads with the B1106 SA. **Take care**. After ¾ km (½ mile) rejoin the first loop, bearing L to return to the start

Useful addresses

British Cycling Federation
National Cycling Centre
Stuart Street
Manchester M11 4DQ
0870 871 2000
www.bcf.uk.com

The BCF co-ordinates and promotes an array of cycle sports and cycling in general. They are a good first point of contact if you want to find out more about how to get involved in cycling. The website provides information on upcoming cycle events and competitions.

CTC (Cyclists Touring Club)
Cotterell House
69 Meadrow
Godalming
Surrey GU7 3HS
01483 417217
www.ctc.org.uk

Britain's largest cycling organisation, promoting recreational and utility cycling. The CTC provides touring and technical advice, legal aid and insurance, and campaigns to improve facilities and opportunities for all cyclists. The website provides details of campaigns and routes and has an online application form.

The London Cycling Campaign
Unit 228
30 Great Guildford Street
London SE1 0HS
020 7928 7220
www.lcc.org.uk

The LCC promotes cycling in London by providing services for cyclists and by campaigning for more facilities for cyclists. Membership of the LCC provides the following benefits: London Cyclist magazine, insurance, legal advice, workshops, organised rides, discounts in bike shops and much more. You can join the LCC on its website.

Sustrans
Head Office
Crown House
37-41 Prince Street
Bristol BS1 4PS
General information line: 0117 929 0888
www.sustrans.org.uk

A registered charity, Sustrans designs and builds systems for sustainable transport. It is best known for its transformation of old railway lines into safe, traffic-free routes for cyclists and pedestrians and wheelchair users. Sustrans is developing the 13,000 km (8000 mile) National Cycle Network on traffic-calmed minor roads and traffic-free paths, to be completed by the year 2005 with major funding from the Millennium Commission.

Veteran Cycle Club
Membership Secretary
31 Yorke Road
Croxley Green
Rickmansworth
Herts WD3 3DW
www.v-cc.org.uk

A very active club, the VCC is concerned with the history and restoration of veteran cycles. Members enjoy organised rides and receive excellent publications relating to cycle history and club news.